Texte und Materialien

der Frau Professor

Hilprecht Collection

of Babylonian Antiquities

im Eigentum der Friedrich-Schiller-Universität Jena

Herausgegeben von
Manfred Krebernik

Band 11

2018

Harrassowitz Verlag · Wiesbaden

Gabriella Spada

Sumerian Model Contracts from the Old Babylonian Period in the Hilprecht Collection Jena

2018

Harrassowitz Verlag · Wiesbaden

Bibliografische Information der Deutschen Nationalbibliothek
Die Deutsche Nationalbibliothek verzeichnet diese Publikation in der Deutschen Nationalbibliografie; detaillierte bibliografische Daten sind im Internet über http://dnb.dnb.de abrufbar.

Bibliographic information published by the Deutsche Nationalbibliothek
The Deutsche Nationalbibliothek lists this publication in the Deutsche Nationalbibliografie; detailed bibliographic data are available in the Internet at http://dnb.dnb.de.

For further information about our publishing program consult our website http://www.harrassowitz-verlag.de

Printed on permanent/durable paper.
Printing and binding: Memminger MedienCentrum AG
Printed in Germany

ISSN 0232-3001
ISBN 978-3-447-11034-1

VORWORT DES HERAUSGEBERS

Der vorliegende Band 11 der Reihe „Texte und Materialien der Frau Professor Hilprecht Collection“ (zur Bandzählung siehe Vorwort zu Band 6) ist den sumerischen „model contracts“ aus altbabylonischer Zeit – nebst ihren Duplikaten in anderen Sammlungen – gewidmet. Ihre Edition hat Dr. Gabriella Spada, eine führende Spezialistin auf diesem Gebiet, übernommen. Sie hat sich selbst um die Finanzierung ihrer Reisen gekümmert und das Editionsprojekt rasch und zielstrebig durchgeführt. Ich danke ihr sehr herzlich für ihr großes Engagement und die gute Zusammenarbeit. Die für den Druck notwendigen Mittel konnten nun zum ersten Mal aus einem kleinen Jahresbudget bestritten werden, das die Friedrich-Schiller-Universität der Sammlung dankenswerterweise bewilligt hat.

Jena, im März 2018 M. Krebernik

PREFACE BY THE AUTHOR

A Marco e Arturo,
i miei compagni di avventura

The edition of this corpus of tablets from the Hilprecht-Sammlung is part of a larger project aimed at the full edition of all extant Old Babylonian model contracts, resulting in a complete analysis of model contracts as a specific typology.

First of all I want to thank here *il mio maestro* Franco D'Agostino, who followed this work of mine from the very beginning with patience and helpfulness.

Financial support of the project was provided partly by the University of Rome, "Sapienza" ("Writing Techniques vs Technologies for Writing – Progetto di Ricerca di Ateneo 2015): special thanks are due to Lorenzo Verderame (ISO, Rome), who gave me the opportunity to participate in the project, focusing on the advanced scribal learning practices of the Old Babylonian period.

I would like to express my deepest gratitude to Manfred Krebernik, Professor of Altorientalistiche Philologie at the Friedrich-Schiller-Universität Jena and Curator of the Hilprecht-Sammlung, who allowed me to study and publish this corpus of school tablets. My gratitude also goes to his valuable assistants, Prof. Dr. Kai Lämmerhit and Dr. Jana Matuszak, who facilitated my visits to the collection.

I am grateful also to Marten Stol, Niek Veldhuis and Ricardo Dorado Puntch, who offered helpful comments and suggestions: their invaluable remarks greatly improved the edition of this volume. Ronald Veenker has revised the English form of the volume and for this (and for his friendship) I want to thank him warmly. Needless to say, I bear the full responsibility for any errors or omissions.

Thanks also to my family and my dearest friends, who have always supported me in all my projects.

Infine grazie al mio Marco perché, insieme ad Arturo, è sempre al mio fianco e fa il tifo per me, qualsiasi cosa succeda.

Cesenatico, March 2018

Gabriella Spada

TABLE OF CONTENT

1. Introduction

1. The texts

This volume presents the edition of a corpus of eleven cuneiform objects, eight tablets and three prisms (two of them in a fragmentary state) recording model contracts.[1] Being part of the first stage of the Old Babylonian scribal curriculum, model contracts were used to train the scribes in the formal patterns of administration and law. Although they were apparently a common element in scribal schooling and several hundreds of such exercises have survived, only a small number of them has been published to date.[2] While they were not functional documents, but simply didactic tools (being stripped of incidental details, such as the list of witnesses and the date), model contracts follow the common patterns of Sumerian contract types and represent a comprehensive assortment of all possible transactions that the ancient Mesopotamian administration might have been required to draw up in the everyday economic life: barley and silver loans; deeds of real estate, field or slave sale; marriage contracts; adoptions, and so on.

The corpus of cuneiform objects here presented includes three of the five types of tablets within the classification first proposed by M. Civil (1969: 27–28; 1979: 5) and later modified by S. Tinney (1999: 160). According to this division, most of the school tablets seem to have belonged to one of five physical categories, grouped according to their shape and format, and identified by a number (Type I, II, III, IV and Prisms), each of which probably represents a particular teaching method.

Nearly all of the cuneiform tablets in the Hilprecht Sammlung have been excavated during the four campaigns at Nippur carried out by the Babylonian Expedition, affiliated with the University of Pennsylvania (1888–1900). Unfortunately, the archaeological context of the finds remains difficult to determine and field records as well as published accounts can offer only some general information.
Most of the Old Babylonian and school archives are said to have been recovered from the southern part of the eastern mound, known as "Tablet Hill" or the Scribal Quarter (Gibson–Hansen–Zettler 1998–2001: 549–550), which has been further investigated by the Joint Expedition, formed by the Oriental Institute of the University of Chicago and the University Museum of the University of Pennsylvania (1948–1952).
The finds of these archaeological campaigns have been divided between the Ottoman authorities and the American excavators, which means that different parts of all archives are dispersed over different continents, and are housed in the cuneiform collections of Istanbul, Philadelphia, Chicago and Jena.
Recently, C. Proust (2008) and A. Goddeeris (2016) have published all the Old Babylonian mathematical tablets (Proust) as well as the legal and administrative documents (Goddeeris) housed in Jena. In particular, the corpus published by Goddeeris was the last large unpublished part of the Old Babylonian archives excavated by the Babylonian Expedition.

---

[1] Except for HS 1752 (text no. 10), which is a fragment of a multi-column tablet containing some legal cases (the nature of which – real or scholastic – is not easy to establish).

[2] For a list of published model contracts see Spada 2014: 1 fn. 6, with the addition of Spada 2012 (one tablet from the Lloyd E. Cotsen Cuneiform Tablets Collection) and Bodine 2015 (six tablets from the Yale Babylonian Collection; cf. also the reviews to his volume in Charpin 2017 and Spada 2017b). For an edition and translations of the corpus of model contracts see the Old Babylonian Model Contracts project (OBMC, http://oracc.org/obmc), directed by G. Spada (in particular, the writer is preparing the edition of the corpus of model contracts housed in the Schøyen Collection, Oslo, and in the Rosen Collection, Cornell University).

2. Organization of the volume

The prisms and the tablets here presented have been arranged according to the classification of the school tablets: first Prisms, then Type I tablets and finally Type II tablets.[3]

After the catalogue, and the concordances of the HS number and the museum numbers of the duplicates, most of which are unpublished, there is the edition of the entire corpus, with transliteration, translation and commentary.[4]
The volume contains extensive indexes of personal names, deities, toponyms and a glossary, not only of the HS texts, but also of their duplicates used in the commentary.
The plates at the end of the volume offer handcopies and photographs of all the HS tablets.

[3] Two tablets, HS 1752 and HS 2916, are not easily assigned to a specific type in the classification of the school exercises.

[4] Four to five Type II tablets present on the reverse one of the advanced lexical lists which were studied in the third phase of the Old Babylonian curriculum. The writer offers here only a transliteration of those lexical extracts, without any translation or commentary (moreover they have not been included in the final indexes); for their full edition see a forthcoming TMH volume by J.C. Crisostomo (*Lexical Texts in the Hilprecht Collection*).

2. Catalogue and Concordance

CATALOGUE

N°	**Museum n°**	**Classification**
1.	HS 1550+	Prism
2.	HS 1851	Prism
3.	HS 2607	Prism
4.	HS 2500a	Type I tablet
5.	HS 1770	Type II tablet
6.	HS 1608 (+HS 2629)	Type II tablet
7.	HS 1808	Type II tablet
8.	HS 1451	Type II tablet
9.	HS 1607 (+HS 2946)	Type II tablet
10.	HS 1752	Unidentified type of tablet
11.	HS 2916	Unidentified type of tablet

Concordance of duplicates (or related texts) to the model contracts:[5]

HS n°	Duplicates (Mus. n°)
1550+	*3N-T567
	CBS 1206 (P230618)
	CBS 8437 (P230746)
	CBS 8868 (P230620)
	CBS 13866 (P229702)
	IM 58639 (P230806)
	MS 4979 (P254010)
	N 950 (P230642)
	N 2469 (228140)
	N 4075 (P230665)
	N 5863 (P229699)
	SLFN 74, 3N-T927, 513 (P230715)
	UM 29-15-617 (P255081)
	UM 55-21-333 (P230711)
1608	A 30173 (P229564)
	CBS 10288 (P230751)
	N 1326 (P230644)
1808	CBS 10311 (P230794)
	*Ist Ni 10108 (P368911)
	N 4567 (P230591)
	UM 29-16-482 (P230765)
1851	CBS 2298 (P230726)
2500a	MS 3176/5 (P342643)
	UM 29-13-408a (P230634)
2607	CBS 8663+ (P230464)
	Ist Ni 1576 (P231446)
	MS 3176/5 (P342643)
	UM 55-21-441 (P230713)

Duplicates (Mus. n°)	TMH 11 n°
*3N-T567	1 (§11)
A 30173	6 (§3, §4)
CBS 1206	1 (§1)
CBS 2298	2 (§2)
CBS 8437	1 (§1)
CBS 8663+	3 (§1)
CBS 8868	1 (§5, §7, §8)
CBS 10288	6 (§3, §4)
CBS 10311	7
CBS 13866	1 (§5)
IM 58639	1 (§8)
Ist Ni 1576	3 (§1)
*Ist Ni 10108	7
MS 3176/5	3 (§1); 4 (§6, §9)
MS 4979	1 (§1, §9)
N 950	1 (§1)
N 1326	6 (§1, §3, §4)
N 2469	1 (§1)
N 4075	1 (§1)
N 4567	7
N 5863	1 (§4, §5)
SLFN 74, 3N-T927, 513	1 (§7, §8)
UM 29-13-408a	4 (§9)
UM 29-15-617	1 (§1)
UM 29-16-482	7
UM 55-21-333	1 (§9)
UM 55-21-441	3 (§1)

[5] Nearly all duplicates are unpublished, with the exception of two, which are marked by an asterisk: 3N-T567 (= Civil 1974–1977: 69–70 fn. 8) and Ist Ni 10108 (= Proust 2007: 352). In brackets the P number of the tablet is quoted: it is an identification number, issued by the Cuneiform Digital Library Initiative (http://cdli.ucla.edu) and recognized by all CDLI and ORACC related projects. The P number may be used to locate the latest edition of that tablet and its photographs.
My transliterations are based entirely on photos available on CDLI, except for the tablets of the Schøyen Collection, which I have personally studied and photographed.

3. The Text Edition:
Transliterations, translations and commentary

1. Prisms

Four or six-sided school prisms typically have one to four columns per side and a hollow central axis, apparently to facilitate the handling of the object once mounted on a stick.[6] Although prisms are also classified as Type I sources in Civil's typology, they are formally quite distinct from multi-column tablets. The quality of the writing inscribed on prisms can be substantially inferior to that of other types of exercise tablets, indicating that prisms either had a different function or were copied by less advanced pupils.[7]

Whereas HS 1851 (no. **2**) and HS 2607 (no. **3**) are merely tiny fragments of two consecutive sides of the original four-sided prisms, HS 1550+ (no. **1**) is much better preserved.

In transliterations the first column indicates the running numbers of the lines through each side of the prism, counted separately in each column; the second column (in bold) indicates the number of the lines in each section (these are referred to by the notes in the commentary); where the surface is broken or eroded, the probable number of lost lines is indicated.

1.

Museum n°: HS 1550+

Plates: 1–4 and 17–20

Measurements: max h. 19.5 cm; base: 9×9 cm

State of preservation: the four-sided prism (a parallelepipedon) consists of nine different fragmentary parts[8] and on two sides (A and D) is badly damaged.

The four sides, each divided into three columns, originally were to include ca. 33–35 lines per column, apart from Side D, where signs appear to be larger: originally, it likely contained ca. 23 lines per column. The approximate number of lines visible (only in traces for the most part) on each side are:

	Col. i.	**Col. ii.**	**Col. iii.**
Side A	13 lines	19 lines	30 lines
Side B	27 lines	35 lines	32 lines
Side C	33 lines	33 lines	21 lines
Side D	21 lines	21 lines	//

[6] There is the possibility that prisms were hung from the ceiling and read by rotating them horizontally; the same device is to be found in the Cylinders of Gudea (on the vertical reading of cuneiform script until the Kassite period see most recently Fitzgerald 2003 and Studevent-Hickman 2007). Probably, this expedient was also used to avoid the damage of such a large surface by the natural expansion and contraction of clay due to the baking and the drying process.

[7] Since "prisms must have been fairly difficult to produce and inscribe", N. Veldhuis (1997: 31) has suggested that "they may have been produced for special occasions, for instance as a kind of examination, which would also account for their relative rarity". For this hypothesis see also Crisostomo 2015: 127–128. For the idea that literary prisms may have been votive offerings cf. Delnero 2013: 146.

[8] The nine separate fragments, which have been joined, are: HS 1550, HS 1551, HS 1614, HS 1724, HS 1850, HS 1865, HS 2510, HS 2634 and HS 2911. The fragment HS 2634 has been recognized as a part of the prism by the present writer during her stay at the Hilprecht Sammlung of the Friedrich-Schiller-Universität of Jena in July 2015.

The collection of the fifteen model contracts preserved on the prism includes nine manumissions of female and male slaves, two rentals of boats, one hire of a slave and another text concerning a slave; unfortunately, the content of the last two contracts is not understandable.

Inner organization of the prism:

Side A

§1	manumission of a slave-girl	i. 1'–12'
§2	manumission of a slave-girl[9]	i. 13'–ii. 10'
§3	manumission of a slave-girl	ii. 11'–iii. 7
§4	manumission of a slave-girl	iii. x+8–x+16
§5	manumission of a slave-girl (continuing in side B)	iii. x+17–x+23

Side B

§5	manumission of a slave-girl	i. 1–14
§6	manumission of a slave	i. 34–ii. 2
§7	manumission of a slave	ii. 3–34
§8	manumission of a slave	ii. 35–iii. 19
§9	manumission of a slave (continuing in side C)	iii. 20–35

Side C

§9	manumission of a slave	i. 1–20
§10	rental of a boat	i. 21–ii. 4
§11	rental of a boat	ii. 5–28
§12	hire of a slave	ii. 29–iii. 22
§13	content not completely identified (slave) (continuing in side D)	iii. 23–31

Side D

§13	content not completely identified (slave)	i. 1–18
§14	content unknown	i. 19–23
§15	content unknown	ii. 1'–21'

[9] Just the first line and the final oath are preserved.

Seven of the entire group of contracts have duplicates,[10] all of them from Nippur,[11] which are found mainly in the cuneiform collection of the University of Pennsylvania.

Contracts on the prism		Duplicates	
§1	Manumission of Ištar-ennam, slave-girl of Lugal-amaru	1.	CBS 1206 (o.i'. 1'–14')
		2.	CBS 8437
		3.	N 950 (o.i'. 1–7)
		4.	N 2469 (o. 1'–9')
		5.	N 4075 (o.ii'. 1'–9')
		6.	UM 29-15-617 (o.ii'. 1–10)
		7.	MS 4979 (o. 1–18)
§4	Manumission of ..., slave-girl of Šāt-Ninurta	1.	*N 5863 (r.ii'. 1'–15')
§5	Manumission of Amat-Šamaš, slave-girl of Šamaš-bāni	1.	*CBS 8868 (r.i'. 1'–9')
		2.	CBS 13866 (r.ii'. 2–16)
		3.	*N 5863 (r.iii'. 1'–17')
§7	Manumission of Iliš-tikal, slave of Ilī-ennam	1.	*CBS 8868 (r.ii'. 3'–10')
		2.	*SLFN 74, 3N-T927, 513 (i'. 1'–7')
§8	Manumission of Abum-waqar, slave of Ninurta-palil	1.	*CBS 8868 (o.i. 1'-14')
		2.	IM 58639 (o.ii'. 1'–10')
		3.	*SLFN 74, 3N-T927, 513 (ii'. 1'–7')
§9	Manumission of ..., slave of Ur-kuzu and Ninḫegal	1.	UM 55-21-333 (o.i. 1'–8')
		2.	MS 4979 (r. 1–18)
§11	Rental of a boat and accessories	1.	3N-T567 (o.i. 1–20)

Three of these duplicates, which are here marked by an asterisk, contain more than one contract of manumission recorded on the prism and seem to follow that same sequence of contracts,[12] which, therefore, appears to be standardized.

[10] That model contracts exist in multiple copies of a single transaction is a predominant feature of this genre (and of the school texts in general).
[11] Except for MS 4979, the provenience of which is unknown. This tablet will be published by the writer together with other model contracts housed in the Schøyen Collection.
[12] In the other duplicates it is not possible to verify the presence of this same sequence since they are fragmentary. For the sequence of exercises in a Type II tablet (as is CBS 8868) see the introduction to this type of tablet on p. 60.

The first nine contracts record the manumission of female and male slaves;[13] manumission was one of the three ways through which slavery could be ended[14] and often took the form of a ceremony during which some symbolic acts occurred.[15]
Old Babylonian documents of manumission record reciprocal arrangements between the slave who is freed in return for continuing to look after his former master, especially in his old age.[16]
These arrangements were of two kinds: in the first, the master manumitted the slave upon his death, in return for support during the rest of his life. In the second one, the manumission with a duty to support the former owner was combined with the adoption of the slave, who was then doubly bound by the duties of the contract and of sonship (cf. Westbrook 1995: 1648–1651).[17]
There is no evidence to support the notion that the adopted slave's freedom was contingent upon the fulfillment of support and other obligations during the adopter's lifetime, and that the slave did not receive his or her freedom until the adopter's death. The formula which prohibits members of the master's family from claiming the manumittee as a slave after the father's death, is not to be interpreted as if the slave was not free until his master's death. Instead, such clauses were probably inserted to protect the manumittee slave from illegal "reclaiming" by the natural sons, who might conceivably deny that the manumission/adoption had even taken place.

§1 (A.i. 1'–12') Manumission of a slave-girl
The first column of this side is almost completely lost and the preserved portion, apparently containing thirteen lines, is badly damaged due to the abraded surface. However, it is possible to restore the first twelve lines visible on the basis of the several duplicates of this manumission contract.

A.i.			[...]
	1'.	**1'.**	*traces*
	2'.	**2'.**	[eĝir lugal-a-m]a-⸢ru⸣
	3'.	**3'.**	[ba-uš$_2$]-⸢a-ta⸣
	4'.	**4'.**	[ibila lugal]-a-ma-ru
	5'.	**5'.**	[a-na m]e-a-⸢bi⸣
	6'.	**6'.**	[^{I}*iš$_8$-tar$_2$-e*]*n*-⸢*nam*-ra⸣
	7'.	**7'.**	[nam-gem]e$_2$-⸢ni⸣-še$_3$
	8'.	**8'.**	[u$_3$ niĝ$_2$-b]a-ni-⸢še$_3$⸣
	9'.	**9'.**	[inim nu-um-ĝ]a$_2$-⸢ĝa$_2$-a⸣
	10'.	**10'.**	[^{I}lugal-a-m]a-⸢ru⸣
	11'.	**11'.**	[ad-d]a ti[l$_3$]-⸢la⸣
	12'.	**12'.**	[mu] lugal-b[i] / ⸢in⸣-pad$_3$

[13] For an analysis of the definition and the terminology of slavery and slaves in the Old Babylonian period cf. Stol 2011: 564–571. See also Gelb 1982, where the author offers a study on the signs expressing the status of a slave.
[14] In addition to the manumission, a slave could be freed through redemption and debt-release (see Westbrook 2003: 384).
[15] For a study of these symbolic acts related to the manumission of a slave see Malul 1988: 40–76.
[16] For an overview about the care of the elderly during the Old Babylonian period see Stol 1998.
[17] For the format of the adoption-manumission documents see Mendelsohn 1949: 78 and Schorr 1913: 43 and 45. According to some scholars (Koschaker 1931: 73–74 and Szlechter 1952: 176ff.), the manumission of slaves was legally effectuated in southern Babylonia by a court declaration (with the immediate total release of the slave) and in northern Babylonia by an act of adoption (and total emancipation would then be effectuated at the death of the master/parent). Contra Koschaker, Driver and Miles (1955: 227–228) suggested that the adoption and manumissions from northern Babylonia were separate actions recorded in one document.

“...$^{10'-11'}$[Lugal-am]aru, [the fathe]r, while alive, $^{12'}$has sworn by [the name] of the king that $^{2'-3'}$[after Lugal-am]aru [will have died, $^{4'-5'}$any heirs of Lugal]-amaru, [how many there may be], $^{9'}$shall [not raise a claim] $^{6'}$against [Ištar-e]nnam $^{7'-8'}$concerning her [status as a slave and] her sh[are (lit. free gift)]”.

Notes

Only the final section of a manumission contract is preserved here. It usually contains the promissory oath (expressed by the generic formula mu lugal-bi in-pad$_3$, without any specific designations of the names of gods and/or the king) and the clause protecting the freed slave against any future claims and forbidding the heirs of the former owner (his relatives and, primarily, his natural children) to raise claims against him/her.

The manumission of a certain Ištar-ennam, the slave-girl of Lugal-amaru, appears in several other copies, some in a very fragmentary condition and with slight textual variations: CBS 1206 (a fragment of a Type I or II tablet), CBS 8437 (Type III tablet), N 950 (a fragment of a Type I tablet), N 2469 (a fragment of an unidentified type of tablet), N 4075 (a fragment of a Type I or II tablet), UM 29-15-617 (a fragment of a Type I or II tablet); to these Nippur tablets is to be added also MS 4979 (a Type III tablet, the provenience of which is unknown).

The transliterations of these texts are offered below, beginning with CBS 8437, the text of which is almost completely preserved.[18] For the reader’s sake, its complete translation is also provided.

Duplicates:

CBS 8437

o.	1.	**1.**	1 saĝ-⸢munus⸣
	2.	**2.**	*iš*$_8$*-tar*$_2$-⸢*en-nam*⸣ mu-ni-[im]
	3.	**3.**	geme$_2$ lugal-⸢a-ma-ru⸣
	4.	**4.**	ama-⸢ar-gi$_4$-ni in-ĝar⸣
	5.	**5.**	saĝ-⸢ki-ni⸣ in-dadag
	6.	**6.**	dug nam-geme$_2$-ni-še$_3$
	7.	**7.**	in-gaz
	8.	**8.**	kišib nam-sikil-la-ni-še$_3$
	9.	**9.**	in-na-an-tak$_4$
	10.	**10.**	1(diš) sar e$_2$ du$_3$-a
	11.	**11.**	⸢e$_2^?$-ad⸣-da-ni-[ka$^?$]
r.	1.	**12.**	1 ^{na4}kinkin zi-⸢bi šu si$_3$-ga⸣
	2.	**13.**	1 ^{ĝeš}banšur-zag-gu-la
	3.	**14.**	1 ^{ĝeš}kuĝ$_5$(I.DIB)
	4.	**15.**	1 ^{ĝeš}muru$_5^!$(SAL.UD.<EDIN>)-za-nu-um
	5.	**16.**	in-na-an-ba
	6.	**17.**	ud til$_3$-la-ni-še$_3$
	7.	**18.**	igi-ni-še$_3$ i$_3$-gub-bu
	8.	**19.**	ud kur$_2$-še$_3$ ibila lugal-a-ma-ru
	9.	**20.**	a-na me-a-bi ^{I}*iš*$_8$*-tar*$_2$*-en-nam*-ra nam-ge[me$_2$-ni-še$_3$]
	10.	**21.**	u$_3$ niĝ$_2$-ba-ni-še$_3$ inim nu-un-ĝa$_2$-[ĝa$_2$-a]
	11.	**22.**	^{I}lugal-a-ma-ru ad-da til$_3$-la
	12.	**23.**	mu lugal-bi in-pad$_3$

[18] See also Spada *forthcoming*.

"^{4}<Lugal-amaru, her master> has freed $^{1–3}$a woman, named Ištar-ennam, the slave-girl of Lugal-amaru; ^{5}he has cleared her forehead, $^{6–7}$smashed the pot of her slavery (and) $^{8–9}$drawn up for her a document concerning her cleaning. ^{16}He has allotted to her $^{10–11}$a built-up house plot of 1 *sar* (= 36 m^2) belonging to his patrimony$^?$, ^{12}one *zību*-millstone provided with a muller, ^{13}one cultic table, ^{14}one ladder, (and) ^{15}one table. $^{17–18}$As long as he (= Lugal-amaru) lives, she will serve him. $^{22–23}$Lugal-amaru, the father, while alive, has sworn by the name of the king that $^{19–21}$in the future, any heirs of Lugal-amaru, how many there may be, shall not raise a claim against Ištar-ennam [concerning her] status as a slave and her share".

12: this term, indicating a type of millstone, was discussed most recently by M. Civil (Civil 2006: 132 and Civil 2008: 77f.). He asserts that zi-bi refers to the type of clay used for molds: ^{na4}kinkin ad-bar would have been made of stone (basalt), ^{na4}kinkin zi-bi of overfired clay. The Sumerian šu indicates here the muller or pounding stone (in Akkadian *narkabu*).
13: in the Nippur and Ur inheritance divisions, the cultic table usually appears in the preferential portion awarded to the eldest brother.[19]
14: ^{ĝeš}I.DIB (and its paleographic variants ^{ĝeš}I.LU and ^{ĝeš}I.EŠ$_2$), to be read as ^{ĝeš}kuĝ$_{4/5}$ in Sumerian, denotes apparently both the threshold (of an outer door) with its step (Akk. *askuppu*) and the steps of a ladder or of a staircase (Akk. *simmiltu*).[20]
15: this Sumerian term, equivalent to Akkadian *murzānu/murzīnu*, indicates a type of table. It is found in various forms in OB Ura: ^{ĝeš}muru$_5$-za-nu-um, ur-za-nu-um, u$_4$-ru-za-nu-um, ^{ĝeš}mur-zi-nu-um, ^{ĝeš}u$_5$-za-nu-um.[21]

CBS 1206 (o.i'. 1'–14')

o.i'.		[...]
1'.	**1'.**	[1 ^{na4}kinkin zi-bi šu s]i$_3$-ga
2'.	**2'**	[in-n]a-an-šum$_2$
3'.	**3'.**	⸢en⸣-na lugal-a-ma-ru
4'.	**4'.**	al-til$_3$-la-aš
5'.	**5'.**	igi-ni-še$_3$ i$_3$-gub-bu
6'.	**6'.**	eĝir lugal-a-ma:ru
7'.	**7'.**	ba-uš$_2$-a-ta
8'.	**8'.**	⸢ibila⸣ lugal-a-ma-ru
9'.	**9'.**	[a]-⸢na⸣ me-a-bi
10'.	**10'.**	[nam]-geme$_2$-ni-še$_3$
11'.	**11'.**	⸢inim⸣ nu-um-ĝa$_2$-ĝa$_2$-a
12'	**12'.**	^{I}lugal-a-ma-ru
13'	**13'.**	ad-da til$_3$-la
14'	**14'.**	mu lugal-la-bi in-pad$_3$

[19] Cf. Charpin 1980: 37–38. For the proposal that in Nippur private homes this cultic table was a sort of altar for the ancestors' worship see Prang 1976: 28. For the so-called "^{ĝeš}banšur-zag-gu-la-clause" in Nippur documentation, cf. Claassens-van Wyk 2013: 74–75.
[20] Cf. CAD A$_2$ *s.v. askuppu*, p. 335 and Veldhuis 1997: 97, fn. 34.
[21] Cf. the Sumerian glossary in DCCLT, *s.v.* murzanum (http://oracc.org/dcclt/sux).

N 950 (o.i’. 1–7)

o.i’.	1.	**1.**	⸢1⸣ saĝ-munus
	2.	**2.**	^{I}*iš$_8$-tar$_2$-en-nam* mu-ni-im
	3.	**3.**	geme$_2$ lugal-a-ma-ru
	4.	**4.**	⸢^{I}⸣lugal-a-ma-ru lugal-a-ni
	5.	**5.**	[am]a-ar-gi$_4$-ni in-ĝar
	6.	**6.**	[sa]ĝ-ki-ni in-dadag
	7.	**7.**	[dug] ⸢nam-geme$_2$-ni-še$_3$ in-gaz⸣
			rest of column missing

N 2469 (o. 1’–9’)

o$^{?}$.			[...]
	1’.	**1’.**	[1 ^{na4}]⸢kinkin zi⸣-[bi šu si$_3$-ga]
	2’.	**2’.**	[1] ^{geš}banšur-zag-gu-[la]
	3’.	**3’.**	[1] ^{geš}⸢kuĝ$_5$⸣(I.⸢DIB$^{?}$⸣)
	4’.	**4’.**	[1] ^{geš}muru$_5$-za-nu-⸢um⸣
	5’.	**5’.**	in-na-an-[šum$_2$]
	6’.	**6’.**	[u]d til$_3$-la-ni-⸢še$_3$⸣
	7’.	**7’.**	[i]gi-ni-še$_3$ i$_3$-gub-[bu]
	8’.	**8’.**	ud kur$_2$-še$_3$ ibila lu[gal-a-ma-ru]
	9’.	**9’.**	[nam-ge]me$_2$-ni-še$_3$ [...]
			rest of tablet missing

N 4075 (o.ii’. 1’–9’)

o.ii’.			[...]
	1’.	**1’.**	[ibila] / ⸢lugal⸣-[a]-⸢ma-ru⸣
	2’.	**2’.**	a-na me-a-bi
	3’.	**3’.**	^{I}*iš$_8$-tar$_2$-en-nam*-ra
	4’.	**4’.**	nam-geme$_2$-ni-še$_3$
	5’.	**5’.**	u$_3$ niĝ$_2$-ba-ni-še$_3$
	6’.	**6’.**	inim nu-um-ĝa$_2$-ĝa$_2$-a
	7’.	**7’.**	^{I}lugal-a-ma-ru
	8’	**8’**	ad-da til$_3$-la
	9’.	**9’.**	mu lugal-bi in-pad$_3$

UM 29-15-617 (o.ii’. 1–10)

o.ii’.	1.	**1.**	1 saĝ-[munus]
	2.	**2.**	[^{I}*iš$_8$*]-*tar$_2$-en-nam*
	3.	**3.**	⸢mu⸣-ni-im
	4.	**4.**	geme$_2$ lugal-a-ma-ru
	5.	**5.**	lugal-a-ma-ru lugal-a-ni
	6.	**6.**	ama-ar-gi$_4$-ni in-ĝar
	7.	**7.**	saĝ-ki-ni in-dadag
	8.	**8.**	dug nam-geme$_2$-ni-še$_3$
	9.	**9.**	⸢in⸣-gaz
	10.	**10.**	[kišib na]m-⸢sikil⸣-[la-ni-še$_3$]
			rest of column missing

MS 4979 (o. 1–18)

o.	1.	**1.**	1 saĝ-munus
	2.	**2.**	^{I}*iš$_8$-tar$_2$-en-nam* mu-ni-im
	3.	**3.**	geme$_2$ lugal-a-ma-ru
	4.	**4.**	lugal-a-ma-ru
	5.	**5.**	lugal-a-ni-⸢ir⸣
	6.	**6.**	ama-ar-gi$_4$-ni in-ĝar
	7.	**7.**	1(diš) sar e$_2$ du$_3$-a
	8.	**8.**	1 ^{na4}kinkin zi-bi šu si$_3$-ga
	9.	**9.**	1 ^{ĝeš}banšur-zag-gu$_2$-la$_2$
	10.	**10.**	1 ^{ĝeš}kuĝ$_5$(I.DIB)
	11.	**11.**	1 ^{ĝeš}muru$_5^!$(UD:SAL.EDIN)-⸢za⸣-nu-um
	12.	**12.**	in-na-an-šum$_2$
	13.	**13.**	ud til$_3$-la-[ni-š]e$_3$
	14.	**14.**	igi-ni-še$_3$ i$_3$-gub-bu
	15.	**15.**	ud kur$_2$-še$_3$
	16.	**16.**	ibila lugal-a-ma-[ru]
	17.	**17.**	nam-geme$_2$-<ni>-še$_3$ u$_3$ niĝ$_2$-⸢ba⸣-ni-<<a-ni>>-[še$_3$]
	18.	**18.**	lugal-a-ma-ru mu lugal-bi in-/pad$_3$

As it will be seen in the following manumission contracts, in the first line the term for "man" or "woman" appears.
For a discussion about the usage of the word saĝ in combination with nita$_{(2)}$ (male), saĝ-nita$_{(2)}$, and munus (female), saĝ-munus, see Steinkeller 1989: 128–131.[22] These terms are commonly translated in the literature as "slave" and "slave-girl" respectively, being considered as a sort of synonymous with arad$_{(2)}$ and geme$_2$. However, Steinkeller argues that their meaning is distinctly different: whereas saĝ-nita$_{(2)}$ and saĝ-munus are basically gender descriptions, arad$_{(2)}$ and geme$_2$ are social classificatory terms. Moreover, he distinguishes saĝ-nita$_{(2)}$ and saĝ-munus also from the terms saĝ-arad$_{(2)}$ and saĝ-geme$_2$, which are standard descriptions of sold humans in Old Babylonian sale documents, and apparently are Old Babylonian creations, due to the loss of the original distinction between saĝ-nita$_{(2)}$/ saĝ-munus and arad$_{(2)}$/geme$_2$.

On the basis of model manumission contracts and of the known real legal documents recording enfranchisement of slaves,[23] it seems that in Nippur this type of documents has the following pattern:

[22] See also Gelb 1982, Farber 2005: 109–112 and Steinert 2012: 175 fn. 162.

[23] To the best of my knowledge, there are six manumission contracts from Old Babylonian Nippur: ARN 7 (dated to Enlil-Bāni f), ARN 62, SAOC 44 53 (Rīm-Sîn 51), PBS 8/2 137 (Samsu-iluna 23), BE 6/2 62 (Samsu-iluna 1; this is a public proclamation of a manumission), TIM 4 15 (Rīm-Sîn 1; its origin from Nippur is not certain), where the individuals to be manumitted are often identified with the generic terms "one man/one woman". In this regard, therefore, it should be reviewed what Veenhof (1982: 375) writes about the repeated use of the terms saĝ-geme$_2$ and geme$_2$ in ARN 7 which, according to him, "reveals problems with the formulary". On the basis of the hand-copy of the tablet, in fact, the first line can be read "1 saĝ-munus" (and not necessarily 1 saĝ-g[eme$_2$]).

1 saĝ-nita$_2$[24]/saĝ-munus	a man/woman,
PN$_1$ mu-ni-im	named PN$_1$,
arad$_{(2)}$[25]/geme$_2$ PN$_2$	(who is) the slave/slave-girl of PN$_2$

Instead, some model contracts from other sites present in the first line the terms saĝ-arad$_{(2)}$/saĝ-geme$_2$ (e.g. Spada 2011, §43: 1).

The basic schematic form of the Old Babylonian Nippur manumission contracts may contain the following elements:[26]

1. freedom-establishing clause
2. ritual action clause(s)
3. document-drafting clause
4. service until master's death
5. no-contest clause
6. oath
7. witnesses
8. date

It seems that between Nippur real documents and school texts there is a structural difference: in model contracts there is always the "PN mu-ni-im" formula, whereas this is not the case in real-life documents. This expression (Akk. *šumšu*) has implications for the person it refers to; it is a reference to the social status of the person, identifying him/her as a slave,[27] and eventually its function can be regarded as similar to that of the patronymic among the free people (David 1927: 69).

§2 (A.i. 13'–ii. 10') Manumission of a slave-girl

A.i.	13'.	**1.**	[1 sa]ĝ-⸢munus⸣
A.ii.			*unknown number of lines missing*
			8 lines unreadable
	9'.	**x+9.**	⸢ad-da⸣ t[il$_3$-l]a
	10'.	**x+10.**	⸢mu lugal-bi⸣ i[n-pa]d$_3$

[24] To the best of my knowledge, all the Old Babylonian model contracts present the ARAD-sign, to be read nita$_2$ in accordance with munus.

[25] Due to the damaged surface of the prism, it is not always easy to distinguish ARAD from ARAD$_2$ (ARAD×KUR) in the contracts recording the manumission of a male slave. When the presence of KUR inside ARAD is certain, then the sign will be read arad$_2$, otherwise it will be merely transliterated arad. There seems to be no hint to any semantic differentiation of these two signs in this type of document.

[26] This schema is valid also for Nippur model manumission contracts, which obviously, being school exercises, are stripped of the list of witnesses and the date (items 7 and 8).

[27] For discussions of its meaning and implications see Schorr 1913: 43–44, David 1927: 68–69 and Ellis 1975: 139–140. For a theory according to which this formula is an indication of the changing of the slave's name during the ritual enslavement see Vandorpe 2010. She proposes to read the clause 1 saĝ-arad/saĝ-geme$_2$ PN mu-ni-im as "one slave/slave-girl from now on being called PN". However, she believes that slaves kept their name after being manumitted, which can explain why one finds certain slave names among free people.

“^{1}A woman [...]. $^{x+9–x+10}$(PN) the father, whi[le ali]ve, ha[s swor]n by the name of the king that [...]”.

Notes

This model contract recording the manumission of a slave-girl begins in the last line of the first column and continues in the second column, which is unfortunately badly damaged. After a large portion of several lines completely lost, it is possible to identify ten final lines of the contract, but only the very last two are readable. The sign traces in the previous eight lines do not seem to match with the formularies that one expects in a manumission contract.

§3 (A.ii. 11’–iii 7) Manumission of a slave-girl

A.ii.	11’.	**1.**	1 ⸢saĝ⸣-[munus]
	12’.	**2.**	⸢^{I}KA-^{d}en-lil$_2$-la$_2$⸣
	13’.	**3.**	⸢mu-ni-im⸣
	14’.	**4.**	⸢geme$_2$ im$^?$-gur$^?$⸣-^{d}nin-urt[a]
	15’.	**5.**	⸢gudug$^?$ ^{d}⸣nin-⸢urta⸣
	16’.	**6.**	⸢dumu$^?$ x⸣-^{d}⸢x-x⸣-ni
	17’.	**7.**	*traces*
	18’	**8.**	*traces*
	19’.	**9.**	[ama]-⸢ar-gi$_4$-ni⸣ in-ĝar
A.iii.	1.	**10.**	[saĝ-ki-ni in-dadag]
	2.	**11.**	[dug na]m-ge[me$_2$-ni-še$_3$]
	3.	**12.**	[i]n-gaz
	4.	**13.**	[kišib n]am-sikil-la-ni-še$_3$
	5.	**14.**	[in-na]-an-tak$_4$
	6.	**15.**	[ud til$_3$-l]a-ni-še$_3$
	7.	**16.**	[igi-ni-še$_3$ i$_3$-g]ub-bu
			rest missing

“(Imgur$^?$-Ninurta, her master), ^{9}has freed $^{1–4}$a wo[man] named KA-Enlila, the slave-girl of Imgur$^?$-Ninurt[a], $^{5–8}$*pašīšum*-priest of Ninurta, son$^?$ of PN, ... ^{10}[he has cleared her forehead], $^{11–12}$smash[ed the pot of her sla]very (and) $^{13–14}$drawn up [for her a document] concerning her cleaning. $^{15–16}$As long as [he (= Imgur$^?$-Ninurta) lives, she will se]rve [him] ...”.

Notes

9: according to Roth (1979: 112–114), it was the ama-ar-gi$_4$ ~ ĝar formula (lit: “to establish [one’s] return to the mother”, corresponding to the Akkadian *andurārum šakānum*, “to establish [one’s] freedom” [28]), which legally effectuated the slave’s freedom, whereas the symbolic acts, which may precede or follow this formula (here listed in the following five lines) were not constitutive elements in the process of manumission.

According to Malul (1988: 63–64) this clause does not represent the constitutive element of manumission, but seems to have the character of a summary remark on the written level describing the status of freedom newly granted to the slave by means of a symbolic ceremony.

[28] D. Charpin (1987: 37) argues that this formula means “retour à la situation originelle”, i.e. the return to the status one has at birth, therefore freedom for the one born free, but slavery to his former master if one is born slave.

10–12: these are two symbolic acts which pertain to manumission of slaves; they may appear both in real-life contracts and in school texts. They are found not only in model contracts but also in school legal phrasebooks, such as OB ki-ulutin-bi-še$_3$ and OB Ura 1 and 2.[29]
The first act is expressed by the Sumerian formula saĝ-ki ~ dadag (Akkadian *pūtam ullulu*/*ubbubu*), "to cleanse, purify the forehead". Since it seems to have been actually performed, Malul suggests that the verb should be understood in its primary meaning ("to cleanse, purify"), rather than its secondary one ("to clear a person or property of legal or financial claims", "to clear oneself of an accusation by means of an oath"; cf. CAD E, p. 6f. *s.v. ubbubu*, meanings c and d).[30] As for the material which may have been used as the cleansing agent in the purification ceremony, it is unclear whether it was oil or water, and the texts are completely silent about it.[31]
The second symbolic act is expressed by the formula dug ~ gaz, (Akkadian *karpatam ḫepû*), "to break the pot (of slavery)", which seems to "break" the old personality, leading to the slave's nullification. All the Old Babylonian model contracts of manumission from Nippur designate the pot to be broken as dug nam-geme$_2$/arad, "the pot of slavery",[32] but the texts do not offer any detail as to the nature of this pot, whether it was an ordinary ceramic ware, or a specific pot manufactured for the occasion of the ceremony.
13–14: southern documents make an explicit reference to a "document of purification" (kišib nam-sikil-la), which appears to have been drawn up regularly after every case of manumission in order to record it.[33] This document, given to the freed slave,[34] probably served not as the actual legal instrument which effectuated the slave's freedom, but rather as evidence to be produced in case the freed status of the slave is challenged by any future claim. For the clause protecting the freed slave against such claims cf. the commentary to §1 above.
For tak$_4$ = *ezēbu*, "to draw up a legal document", see Ai. VI iv 11–12[35] and CAD E, *s.v. ezēbu* 3d, p. 422.
15–16: this formula, which may be compared with Akkadian *maḫar* PN *izuzzu* (cf. CAD U/W, *s.v. uzuzzu*, p. 382f.),[36] expresses the obligation of the person manumitted "to stay before, to remain at the order of" his former owner, i.e. to support him for life. Therefore the slave, though legally free, still remains in a state of dependency and becomes completely free only after the death of his former master. The clause described here does not imply adoption, but through it the manumitter secures himself of the services of his former slave during his old age. Such services could eventually be rewarded by inheritance rights, after the death of the former owner,[37] as it is clear from the manumission contracts §1 (and its duplicates) and §5 (see below).

---

[29] For a study of these symbolic acts related to the manumission of a slave see Malul 1988: 40–76.
[30] Cf. also Steinert 2012: 203f.
[31] Malul (1988: 46–47) has suggested the employment of oil, based on parallels with a later manumission text from Ugarit and the Middle Assyrian Epic of Tukulti-Ninurta.
[32] This designation appears also in three real-life contracts (BE 6/2 8; PBS 8/2 137; SAOC 44 53).
[33] See e.g. PBS 8/2 137, which is labeled "document of purification"; cf. Roth 1979: 106.
[34] Cf. Spada 2011 §40 5'–6'.
[35] ^{na4}kišib min$_3$-kam$_2$-ma in-na-an-tak$_4$ / *ku-nu-ka ša-nam-ma i-zi-ib-šu*.
[36] For the use of the verb *wašābu* in this formula cf. CT 48 57: 22f.
[37] In Sippar, differently from normal adoption contracts, the former slave never inherits property from the adoptive parent (cf. Harris 1975: 347).

The prism is broken here and, after an unknown number of lines missing, there are twenty-three lines visible. However, the first seven lines are very damaged and are impossible to read.

§4 (A.iii. x+8–x+16) Manumission of a slave-girl

A.iii.			[...]
	x+8.	**1'.**	⸢eĝir-ra *ša*⸣-*at*-^{d}n[in-urta]
	x+9.	**2'.**	⸢ba⸣-uš$_{2}$-a-t[a]
	x+10.	**3'.**	⸢ibila *ša*⸣-*at*-⸢^{d}⸣n[in-urta]
	x+11.	**4'.**	⸢a-na⸣ m[e-a-bi]
	x+12.	**5'.**	n[am]-gem[e$_{2}$-ni-še$_{3}$]
	x+13.	**6'.**	⸢inim⸣ nu-u[m-ĝa$_{2}$-ĝa$_{2}$-a]
	x+14.	**7'.**	^{I}⸢*ša*⸣-*at*-⸢^{d}⸣[nin-urta]
	x+15.	**8'.**	⸢ama⸣ til$_{3}$-[la]
	x+16.	**9'.**	⸢mu lugal⸣-[b]i i[n-pad$_{3}$]

"[...] $^{7'–9'}$Šāt-[Ninurta], the mother, while al[ive], ha[s sworn] by the name of the king that $^{1'–2'}$after Šāt-N[inurta] will have died, $^{3'–4'}$any heirs of Šāt-N[inurta], how many there may be, $^{5'–6'}$shall not [raise] a claim [concerning her] status as a slav[e-girl]".

Notes

The preserved portion of the contract is the final section of a manumission contract which is also found in a Type II tablet, N 5863, recording proverbs on the obverse and model contracts on the reverse (see also §5 below). In particular, N 5863 preserves the central part of the contract, including also the supporting clause for the benefit of the former mistress (for this clause see §7 in the prism and text no. 9 below).

Duplicate:

N 5863 (r.ii'. 1'–15')

r.ii'.	1'.	**1'.**	s[aĝ-ki-ni in-dadag]
	2'.	**2'.**	d[ug nam-geme$_{2}$-ni-še$_{3}$]
	3'.	**3'.**	i[n-gaz]
	4'.	**4'.**	kišib [nam-sikil-la-ni-še$_{3}$]
	5'.	**5'.**	in-na-[an-tak$_{4}$]
	6'.	**6'.**	ud til$_{3}$-⸢la⸣-ni-[še$_{3}$]
	7'.	**7'.**	igi-ni-še$_{3}$ i$_{3}$-gu[b-bu]
	8'.	**8'.**	iti-da 4(ban$_{2}$) zid$_{2}$-gu-ta-[am$_{3}$]
	9'.	**9'.**	$^{2}/_{3}$ sila$_{3}$ i$_{3}$-⸢ĝeš⸣-ta-am$_{3}$
	10'.	**10'.**	mu-am$_{3}$ 6 ma-na siki-ta-/am$_{3}$
	11'.	**11'.**	še-ba i$_{3}$-ba ⸢u$_{3}$⸣ siki-ba
	12'.	**12'.**	^{I}*ša-at*-^{d}nin-urta
	13'.	**13'.**	nin-a-ni-ir
	14'.	**14'.**	in-⸢na$^{?}$-ab$^{?}$⸣-kalag-⸢ge⸣
	15'.	**15'.**	⸢x x x⸣ [x]
			rest of column missing

"(Šāt-Ninurta, her mistress, has freed a woman named PN); $^{1'}$[she has cleared her forehe]ad, $^{2'–3'}$sm[ashed the pot of her slavery] (and) $^{4'–5'}$[drawn up] for her a document [concerning her cleaning]. $^{6'–7'}$As long as she (= Šāt-Ninurta) lives, she will serve her. $^{12'–14'}$She will provide Šāt-

Ninurta, her mistress, [8'–11']monthly 4 *ban* (= 40 litres) of flour, $^2/_3$ *sila* of oil (and) annually 6 minas of wool, (as her) barley, oil and wool rations [...]".

§5 (A.iii. x+17–B.i. 14) Manumission of a slave-girl

A.iii.	x+17.	**1.**	⸢1⸣ [s]aĝ-m[unus]
	x+18.	**2.**	[^{I}gem]e$_2$-^{d}⸢utu⸣
	x+19.	**3.**	mu-ni-⸢im⸣
	x+20.	**4.**	geme$_2$ ^{d}⸢utu⸣-*ba-ni*
	x+21.	**5.**	⸢^{Id}utu⸣-*ba-n*[*i*]
	x+22.	**6.**	lugal-a-ni-⸢ir⸣
	x+23.	**7.**	ama-ar-gi$_4$-⸢ni⸣ / i[n-ĝar]
B.i.	1.	**8.**	[saĝ-ki-ni in]-⸢dadag⸣
	2.	**9.**	[dug nam-ge]me$_2$-ni-še$_3$
	3.	**10.**	[i]n-gaz
	4.	**11.**	kišib nam-sikil-la-ni-še$_3$
	5.	**12.**	in-na-an-tak$_4$
	6.	**13.**	⸢1(diš)⸣ s[ar] ⸢e$_2$⸣ du$_3$-a
	7.	**14.**	d[a e$_2$ *i*$_3$]-*li*$_2$-*pu-uṭ-ra-am*
	8.	**15.**	[kug-ta sa$_{10}$]-⸢am$_3$⸣
	9.	**16.**	[ki lu$_2$-ti-la-DI si]mug$^?$
	10.	**17.**	[5(iku) GAN$_2$ a-šag$_4$ ba]n$_3$-da
	11.	**18.**	[kug-ta] sa$_{10}$-a[m$_3$]
	12.	**19.**	[ki *i-din*]-*iš*$_8$-*tar*$_2$
	13.	**20.**	[...] ⸢x⸣-bi$^?$
	14.	**21.**	[...] ⸢x⸣
			rest broken

"[5–7]Šamaš-bān[i], her master, has freed [1–4]a wo[man], named [Ama]t-Šamaš, the slave-girl of Šamaš-bāni; [8]he has cleared [her forehead], [9–10]smashed [the pot] of her sla[very] (and) [11–12]drawn up for her a document concerning her cleaning. (He has allotted to her) [13–16]a built-up house plot of 1 *sar* (= 36 m^2), ne[xt to the house of I]lī-puṭram, bo[ught from LutilaDI, the sm]ith, [17–19][5 *iku* (= 1.8 ha.) of the "sma]ll [field"] bought [from Iddin]-Ištar, ..."

Notes

14–19: these fragmentary lines are restored on the basis of two duplicates, which are contained in one Type I tablet, CBS 13866, and one Type II tablet, N 5863 (see above); apparently another duplicate occurs in CBS 8868 (maybe a Type II tablet, recording model contracts on both sides).
16: to the best of my knowledge, a similar personal name appears only in one tablet from Larsa (YOS 5, 125 r. 3): lu$_2$-ti-la-DI-bi.
17: this field is listed in the OB Nippur Ura 5 69 (see MSL 11 98). Cf. also Goddeeris 2016, text 41.

Duplicates:

CBS 13866 (r.ii’. 2–16)

r.ii’.	2.	**1.**	1 saĝ-munus
	3.	**2.**	geme$_2$-^{d}utu mu-ni-i[m]
	4.	**3.**	geme$_2$ ^{d}utu-*ba-ni*
	5.	**4.**	^{Id}utu-*ba-ni* lugal-a-ni
	6.	**5.**	ama-ar-gi$_4$-ni in-ĝar
	7.	**6.**	saĝ-ki-ni in-dadag
	8.	**7.**	dug nam-geme$_2$-⸢ni⸣-še$_3$ in-gaz
	9.	**8.**	⸢kišib⸣ nam-sikil-la-⸢ni⸣-še$_3$
	10.	**9.**	in-na-an-tak$_4$
	11.	**10.**	1(diš) sar e$_2$ du$_3$-a
	12.	**11.**	da e$_2$ *i$_3$-li$_2$-pu-uṭ-ra-*/[*am*]
	13.	**12.**	kug-ta ⸢sa$_{10}$-am$_3$⸣ ki ⸢lu$_2$-ti-la⸣-/DI-⸢ta⸣
	14.	**13.**	5(iku) GAN$_2$ a-⸢šag$_4$ ban$_3$⸣-da
	15.	**14.**	[...] ⸢x x⸣
	16.	**15.**	[...] ⸢x x x⸣
			rest of column missing

N 5863 (r.iii’. 1’–17’)

r.iii’.	1’.	**1.**	[1 saĝ-munus]
	2’.	**2.**	[geme$_2$-^{d}utu] mu-ni-[im]
	3’.	**3.**	geme$_2$ ⸢^{d}⸣utu-*ba*-[*ni*]
	4’.	**4.**	^{Id}⸢utu-*ba-ni* lugal⸣-a-ni
	5’.	**5.**	ama-⸢ar-gi$_4$⸣-ni in-ĝar
	6’.	**6.**	saĝ-ki-ni in-dadag
	7’.	**7.**	[dug] nam-geme$_2$-ni-še$_3$
	8’.	**8.**	[in]-gaz
	9’.	**9.**	kišib nam-sikil-la-ni-še$_3$
	10’.	**10.**	in-na-an-tak$_4$
	11’.	**11.**	1(diš) sar e$_2$ du$_3$-a
	12’.	**12.**	da e$_2$ *i$_3$-li$_2$-pu-uṭ-ra-/am*
	13’.	**13.**	kug-ta sa$_{10}$-am$_3$
	14’.	**14.**	ki lu$_2$-ti-la-DI simug-ta
	15’.	**15.**	5(iku) GAN$_2$ a-šag$_4$ ban$_3$-da
	16’.	**16.**	kug-ta sa$_{10}$-am$_3$
	17’.	**17.**	ki *i-din-iš$_8$-tar$_2$*-[t]a
			rest of column missing

CBS 8868 (r.i’. 1’–9’)

r.i’.	1’.	**1’.**	ge[me$_2$ ^{d}utu-*ba-ni*]
	2’.	**2’.**	^{Id}⸢utu⸣-[*ba-ni*]
	3’.	**3’.**	lugal-a-n[i]
	4’.	**4’.**	ama-ar-g[i$_4$-ni] / i[n-ĝar]
	5’.	**5’.**	saĝ-ki-ni [in-dadag]
	6’.	**6’.**	dug nam-[geme$_2$-ni-še$_3$]
	7’.	**7’.**	in-g[az]

	8'.	**8'.**	kišib nam-si[kil-la-ni-še$_3$]
	9'.	**9'.**	i[n-na-an-tak$_4$]
			rest of column missing

The column has a gap of approximately nineteen lines; in ten of them scattered traces of signs are visible. Then, there are the last three lines of the column, which probably represent the final section of a separate manumission contract, since the object of the no-contest clause (lines 34–35) is a male slave.

§6 (B.i. 34–ii. 2) Manumission of a slave

B.i.			[...]
	34.	**6'.**	[na]m-⸢arad⸣-da-ni-še$_3$
	35.	**7'.**	[ini]m nu-⸢um⸣-ĝa$_2$-ĝa$_2$-a
	36.	**8'.**	⸢x-x-x-NI$^?$⸣
B.ii.	1.	**9'.**	[ad-da til$_3$-la$^?$]
	2.	**10'.**	⸢mu lugal-bi⸣ [in-pad$_3$]

"[...] $^{8'-10'}$PN, [the father, while alive, has sworn] by the name of the king that (any heirs of PN) $^{6'-7'}$shall not raise [a claim] concerning his [sta]tus as a slave".

§7 (B.ii. 3–34) Manumission of a slave

B.ii.	3.	**1.**	1 ⸢saĝ⸣-ni[ta$_2$]
	4.	**2.**	^{I}⸢*i$_3$-li$_2$-iš-ti-kal$_2$*⸣
	5.	**3.**	⸢mu-ni-im⸣
	6.	**4.**	arad$_2$ *i$_3$-li$_2$*-⸢*en-nam*⸣
	7.	**5.**	^{I}*i$_3$-li$_2$*-⸢*en*⸣-*nam*
	8.	**6.**	lugal-a-n[i]-ir
	9.	**7.**	⸢ama-ar-gi$_4$⸣-[ni] ⸢in⸣-ĝar
	10.	**8.**	saĝ-ki-⸢ni⸣ i[n]-dadag
	11.	**9.**	^{I}*i$_3$-li$_2$-iš-ti*-⸢*kal$_2$*⸣
	12.	**10.**	ud til$_3$-⸢la⸣-n[i]-še$_3$
	13.	**11.**	iti-⸢da⸣ 2(ban$_2$) še-t[a-a]m$_3$
			6 lines with scattered traces
	20.	**18.**	[*i$_3$-li$_2$-iš*]-*ti*-⸢*kal$_2$*-e$^?$⸣
	21.	**19.**	[...] ⸢in$^?$⸣-na-ab-/⸢kalag⸣-ge
	22.	**20.**	k[išib]-a-ni
	23.	**21.**	al-⸢ze$_2$-er⸣
	24.	**22.**	nam-⸢arad-da⸣-ni-še$_3^!$
	25.	**23.**	ba-⸢ze$_2$⸣-e[r]
	26.	**24.**	eĝir-ra *i$_3$-li$_2$-e*[*n-nam*]
	27.	**25.**	ba-uš$_2$-a-[ta]
	28.	**26.**	[ibil]a ⸢*i$_3$-li$_2$*⸣-*e*[*n-nam*]
	29.	**27.**	[a-na me-a-b]i
	30.	**28.**	n[am-arad-da-n]i-⸢še$_3$⸣
	31.	**29.**	⸢inim nu-um⸣-[ĝa$_2$]-ĝa$_2$-a
	32.	**30.**	⸢^{I}*i$_3$*⸣-*li$_2$*-⸢*en*⸣-*nam*
	33.	**31.**	⸢ad-da til$_3$-la⸣
	34.	**32.**	⸢mu lugal⸣-bi / in-⸢pad$_3$⸣

“[5–7]Ilī-ennam, his master, has freed [1–4]a man named Iliš-tikal, the slave of Ilī-ennam, [8](and) has cleared his forehead. [9–10]Iliš-tikal, as long as he (= Ilī-ennam) lives, [19]will provide him [11]a monthly ration of 2 *ban* (= 20 litres) of barley, [...]. [20–21]Once his do[cument (of slavery)] has been broken, [22–23]his status as a slave will have been canceled.
[30–32]Ilī-ennam, the father, while alive, has sworn by the name of the king that [24–25]after Ilī-en[nam] will have died, [26–27]a[ny heirs] of Ilī-en[nam, how many there may be], [28–29]shall not raise a claim concerning h[is status as a slave]”.

Notes
Partial duplicates of this contract appear also in CBS 8868 (maybe a Type II tablet, see §5 above) and SLFN 74, 3N-T927, 513 (a small fragment of a prism).
19: the verb used here to express the support of the manumitted slave towards his former owner is kalag, which literally means “to make strong”, possibly “to fix”.
The allowance almost invariably consists of rations of barley, wool and oil. A reasonable minimum subsistence level was 2 litres of barley per day, which means 720 litres per year: this is the figure that we find most often. Oil and wool are of minor importance (Stol 1998: 64). In the present case, however, the barley ration seems to be poorer, being 20 litres per month, or just 240 litres per year, i.e. one third of the standard amount.

Duplicates:

CBS 8868 (r.ii’. 3’–10’)

r.ii’.	3’.	**1.**	1 saĝ-nita$_2$
	4’.	**2.**	^{I}*i*$_3$-*li*$_2$-*iš-ti-kal*$_2$
	5’.	**3.**	mu-ni-im
	6’	**4.**	arad$_2$ *i*$_3$-*li*$_2$-*en-nam*
	7’	**5.**	^{I}*i*$_3$-*li*$_2$-*en-nam*
	8’.	**6.**	lugal-a-ni
	9’.	**7.**	ama-ar-gi$_4$-ni / in-ĝar
	10’.	**8.**	[saĝ]-ki-[ni] in-dadag
			rest of column missing

SLFN 74, 3N-T927, 513 (i’. 1’–7’)

i’.	1’.	**1.**	[1 saĝ]-⸢nita$_2$⸣
	2’.	**2.**	[^{I}*i*$_3$-*li*$_2$-*iš-t*]*i-kal*$_2$
	3’.	**3.**	[mu]-ni-im
	4’	**4.**	[arad *i*$_3$-*li*$_2$]-*en-nam*
	5’	**5.**	[^{I}*i*$_3$-*li*$_2$-*en-n*]*am* lugal-a-ni
	6’.	**6.**	[ama-ar-gi$_4$-ni] ⸢in⸣-ĝar
	7’.	**7.**	[saĝ-ki-ni in-da]dag
			rest of column missing

§8 (B.ii. 35–iii. 19) Manumission of a slave

B.ii.	35.	**1.**	1 saĝ-nita$_2$
B.iii.	1.	**2.**	[^{I}*a-bu-um-wa-qar*]
	2.	**3.**	⸢mu-ni⸣-[im]
	3.	**4.**	arad$_2$ ^{d}nin-urta-pa[lil]
	4.	**5.**	^{Id}nin-urta-palil

5.	**6.**	lugal-a-ni
6.	**7.**	ama-ar-gi$_{4}$-ni / in-ĝar
7.	**8.**	saĝ-ki-ni in-dadag
8.	**9.**	^{I}*a-bu-um-wa-qar*
9.	**10.**	ud til$_{3}$-la-ni-še$_{3}$
10.	**11.**	igi-ni-še$_{3}$ i$_{3}$-gub-bu
11.	**12.**	eĝir-⌜ra ^{d}⌝nin-urta-palil
12.	**13.**	ba-uš$_{2}$-a-ta
13.	**14.**	⌜ibila⌝ ^{d}nin-urta-palil
14.	**15.**	a-na me-a-bi
15.	**16.**	nam-arad$_{2}$-da-⌜ni-še$_{3}$⌝
16.	**17.**	[ini]m nu-um-ĝa$_{2}$-⌜ĝa$_{2}$-a⌝
17.	**18.**	⌜^{Id}nin⌝-[urta-palil]
18.	**19.**	⌜ad-da⌝ [til$_{3}$-la]
19.	**20.**	[mu lugal-bi] / ⌜in-pad$_{3}$⌝

"$^{5–7}$Ninurta-palil, his master, has freed $^{1–4}$a man named [Abum-waqar], the slave of Ninurta-pa[lil], ^{8}(and) has cleared his forehead. $^{9–11}$Abum-waqar, as long as he (= Ninurta-palil) lives, will serve him. $^{18–20}$Nin[urta-palil], the father, [while alive], has sworn [by the name of the king that] $^{12–13}$after Ninurta-palil will have died, $^{14–15}$any heirs of Ninurta-palil, how many there may be, $^{16–17}$shall not raise a claim concerning his status as a slave".

Notes

Three duplicates of this contract appear in CBS 8868, SLFN 74, 3N-T927, 513 (both of them contain also duplicates of the previous manumission, §7) and IM 58639 (a fragment of a Type I or II tablet).

Duplicates:

CBS 8868 (o.i. 1'–14')

o.i.			*3 lines missing*
	1'.	**4.**	[^{Id}nin-ur]ta-⌜palil⌝ [lugal-a-ni]
	2'.	**5.**	ama-ar-gi$_{4}$-ni i[n-ĝar]
	3'.	**6.**	saĝ-ki-ni in-da[dag]
	4'.	**7.**	dug nam-arad$_{2}$-da-ni i[n-gaz]
	5'.	**8.**	kišib nam-sikil-la-ni-[še$_{3}$]
	6'.	**9.**	in-na-an-ta[k$_{4}$]
	7'.	**10.**	^{I}*a-bu-um-wa-qar* ud til$_{3}$-la-ni-[še$_{3}$]
	8'.	**11.**	igi-ni-še$_{3}$ i$_{3}$-gub-b[u]
	9'.	**12.**	eĝir-ra ^{d}nin-urta-pa[lil ba-uš$_{2}$-a-ta]
	10'.	**13.**	ibila ^{d}nin-urta-⌜palil⌝
	11'.	**14.**	a-na me-a-[bi]
	12'.	**15.**	nam-arad$_{2}$-da-ni-[še$_{3}$]
	13'.	**16.**	inim nu-um-ĝa$_{2}$-[ĝa$_{2}$-a]
	14'.	**17.**	[^{Id}nin]-urta-palil [ad-da til$_{3}$-la]
			rest of column missing

IM 58639 (o.ii'. 1'–10')

o.ii'.			*2 lines missing*
	1'.	**3.**	⸢mu-ni⸣-[im]
	2'.	**4.**	arad ^{d}ni[n-urta-palil]
	3'.	**5.**	^{Id}nin-urta-[palil] / lugal-a-[ni]
	4'.	**6.**	ama-ar-gi$_4$-[ni in-ĝar]
	5'.	**7.**	saĝ-ki-ni in-[dadag]
	6'.	**8.**	^{I}*a-bu-um-wa-*[*qar*]
	7'.	**9.**	ud til$_3$-[la-ni-še$_3$]
	8'.	**10.**	igi-ni-še$_3$ i$_3$-[gub-bu]
	9'.	**11.**	eĝir ^{d}n[in-urta-palil]
	10'.	**12.**	⸢ba⸣-[uš$_2$-a-ta]
			rest of column missing

SLFN 74, 3N-T927, 513 (ii'. 1'–7')

ii'.			*1 line missing*
	1'.	**2.**	⸢^{I}*a*⸣-[*bu-um-wa-qar*]
	2'.	**3.**	⸢mu-ni⸣-[im]
	3'.	**4.**	arad ^{d}nin-urta-[palil]
	4'.	**5.**	^{Id}nin-urta-palil
	5'.	**6.**	lugal-a-ni
	6'.	**7.**	ama-ar-gi$_4$-ni
	7'.	**8.**	in-⸢ĝar⸣
			rest of column missing

§9 (B.iii. 20–C.i. 20) Manumission of a slave

B.iii.	20.	**1.**	^{I}DIĜIR-⸢x-ma⸣
	21.	**2.**	⸢kur-ra⸣ tu-da
	22.	**3.**	⸢dumu⸣ ir$_3$-^{d}nin-urta / ⸢IM⸣^{ki}
	23.	**4.**	*traces*
			3 lines missing
	27	**8.**	*traces*
	28.	**9.**	^{I}⸢ur-ku$_3$⸣-zu
	29.	**10.**	⸢lugal-a⸣-ni
	30.	**11.**	⸢u$_3$ nin-ḫe$_2$-ĝal$_2$⸣
	31.	**12.**	⸢ama-ar⸣-gi$_4$-ni
	32.	**13.**	in-ĝar-re-⸢ne⸣
	33.	**14.**	⸢en⸣-na ur-⸢ku$_3$-zu⸣
	34.	**15.**	lugal-a-ni
	35.	**16.**	u$_3$ nin-⸢ḫe$_2$-ĝal$_2$⸣
C.i.	1.	**17.**	[nin-a-ni]
	2.	**18.**	⸢na⸣-an-ga-⸢til$_3$-la⸣
	3.	**19.**	⸢igi⸣-ne-ne-še$_3$
	4.	**20.**	i$_3$-gub-bu-<<uš>>
	5.	**21.**	[e]ĝir-ra ur-ku$_3$-zu
	6.	**22.**	[lu]gal-a-ni
	7.	**23.**	⸢u$_3$⸣ nin-ḫe$_2$-ĝal$_2$
	8.	**24.**	[n]in-a-ni

9. **25.** ba-ug$_7$-a-ta
10. **26.** [ib]ila ur-ku$_3$-zu
11. **27.** ⸢u$_3$⸣ nin-ḫe$_2$-ĝal$_2$
12. **28.** ⸢a⸣-na me-a-bi
13. **29.** ⸢nam⸣-arad$_2$-da-ni-še$_3$
14. **30.** ⸢inim⸣ nu-um-ĝa$_2$-ĝa$_2$-ne
15. **31.** ⸢^{I}ur⸣-ku$_3$-zu
16. **32.** ⸢ad⸣-da til$_3$-la
17. **33.** u$_3$ nin-ḫe$_2$-ĝal$_2$
18. **34.** [d]am$^?$ til$_3$-la
19. **35.** mu lugal-bi
20. **36.** in-pad$_3$-de$_3$-eš

"$^{9–13}$Ur-kuzu, his master, and Ninḫegal have freed $^{1–3}$PN, born in a foreign country, the son of Ir-Ninurta of (the city of) IM... $^{14–20}$As long as Ur-kuzu, his master and Ninḫegal [his mistress] live, he will serve them. $^{31–36}$Ur-kuzu, the father, while alive, and Ninḫegal, (his) wife, while alive, have sworn by the name of the king that $^{21–25}$after Ur-kuzu, his master, and Ninḫegal, his mistress, will have died, $^{26–28}$any heirs of Ur-kuzu and Ninḫegal, how many there may be, $^{29–30}$shall not raise a claim concerning his status as a slave".

Notes

Duplicates of this manumission contract appear in a Type II tablet, UM 55-21-333, and (with slight differences in formulary) in a Type III tablet, MS 4979.

2: this line has been tentatively reconstructed based on the signs preserved in MS 4979 r. 2.

3: IM^{ki} is interpreted as a logogram for three different places: Enegi, near Larsa and Uruk, Karkar between Umma and Adab, and Murum, south of Badtibira; cf. Edzard 1976–1980 and Groneberg 1980: 108f. *s.v.* IM.

Duplicates:

UM 55-21-333 (o.i. 1'–8')

o.i. [...]
1'. **1'.** ⸢ibila⸣ [ur-ku$_3$-zu]
2'. **2'.** u$_3$ nin-ḫe$_2$-ĝ[al$_2$]
3'. **3'.** a-na me-a-b[i]
4'. **4'.** nam-arad$_2$-da-ni-[še$_3$]
5'. **5'.** inim nu-um-ĝa$_2$-ĝa$_2$-ne
6'. **6'.** ^{I}ur-ku$_3$-zu ad-d[a] / til$_3$-la
7'. **7'.** u$_3$ nin-ḫe$_2$-ĝal$_2$ ⸢dam$^?$ til$_3$⸣-la
8'. **8'.** mu lugal-bi / in-⸢pad$_3$-/de$_3$-eš⸣

MS 4979 (r. 1–18)

r. 1. **1.** ^{I}DIĜIR-⸢x⸣-ma
2. **2.** ⸢kur-ra tu⸣-da
3. **3.** du[mu ir$_3$-^{d}nin]-⸢urta⸣ IM^{ki}
4. **4.** [... ur-ku$_3$]-zu
8 lines effaced
13. **13.** [ibila$^?$ ur]-⸢ku$_3$⸣-zu-ke$_4$-ne
14. **14.** [...]-⸢x-x⸣

15.	**15.**	[...]-⸢na-de$_2$⸣$^?$-e-ne-a
16.	**16.**	ur-ku$_3$-zu [l]ugal-a-ni-ir
17.	**17.**	u$_3$ nin-[ḫ]e$_2$-ĝal$_2$ nin-a-ni
18.	**18.**	mu lugal-bi in-pad$_3$-eš

§10 (C.i. 21–ii. 4) Rental of a boat

C.i.	21.	**1.**	1 ^{ĝeš}ma$_2$ 2(u)-gur
	22.	**2.**	[1 ^{ĝ}]^{eš}zi-gan
	23.	**3.**	[3$^?$] ⸢^{ĝeš}⸣gi-muš
	24.	**4.**	[1$^?$]+⸢1 eš$_2$⸣ ma$_2$-gid$_2$-da
	25.	**5.**	^{ĝeš}⸢ma$_2$⸣ ^{d}utu/-ma-an-šum$_2$
	26.	**6.**	[du]mu *i$_3$-li$_2$-i-din-nam*
	27.	**7.**	[ki] ^{d}utu-ma-an-šum$_2$
	28.	**8.**	^{I}ir$_{11}$-^{d}imin-⸢bi-ke$_4$⸣
	29.	**9.**	a$_2$ mu-u$_2$-a-še$_3$
	30.	**10.**	[x] ⸢še gur⸣ in-ḫuĝ
	31.	**11.**	[iti ...]-ka
	32.	**12.**	[^{ĝeš}ma$_2$ silim]-ma
	33.	**13.**	[u$_3$] ⸢a$_2$⸣-bi
C.ii.	1.	**14.**	⸢kar-bi⸣-[še$_3$]
	2.	**15.**	⸢gur-ru⸣-[dam]
	3.	**16.**	⸢lu$_2$⸣-ki-ini[m-ma]
	4.	**17.**	iti-bi mu-b[i]

"^{8}Warad-Sebetti ^{10}has rented ^{7}[from] Utu-manšum $^{9–10}$at the annual rent of [x] *gur* of barley $^{1–4}$one boat of 20 *gur* capacity, [one] rudder, [three$^?$] punting poles, [tw]o$^?$ ropes for towing the boat: $^{5–6}$(this is) the boat of Utu-manšum, son of Ilī-iddinam. $^{11–15}$[The boat must be] returned [in good condition, together with] its rent, [at] its quay in the [... month]. $^{16–17}$(Its) witnesses, its month, its year".

Notes

1: the capacity of a boat was calculated with the formula ma$_2$ *x* gur "boat (with the capacity of holding) *x gur*" (cf. OB Nippur Ura 1: 279–286).[38] From the administrative texts we learn of boats from 10 to 120 *gur*, with some smaller (1 and 5 *gur*) and a few larger ones (300 and 360 *gur*) occasionally mentioned. Boats of 60 *gur* appear to be the most prevalent, with 10, 20 and 120 *gur* boats also relatively frequent. It is unclear whether the "*gur*" figure, which in the case of boat sizes may have denoted a unit of mass rather than volume, refers to the total volume of the boat, the volume of cargo carried, the mass displacement of the boat, or the mass of the cargo.[39]

2–4: the hire of a boat is sometimes comprehensive of some accessories for shipping,[40] in this case one rudder (Sumerian ^{ĝeš}zi-gan, equated to the Akkadian *sikkannu*), some boat poles and some ropes for towing the boat (Sumerian eš$_2$ ma$_2$-gid$_2$-da, equated to the Akkadian *massaku*). The Sumerian term ^{ĝeš}gi-muš, here translated as "punting pole", is equated to the Akkadian *gimuššu* and *parrisu* in Ura 4 407–408 (MSL 5: 184). These objects, made of u$_3$-suh$_5$ wood

[38] See the edition in DCCLT: http://oracc.org/dcclt/Q000039.

[39] See Vosmer 2008: 230–231; the author concluded that it must refer to the volume or mass of the cargo alone.

[40] E.g. UET 5 224, 228–230.

(maybe a local pine, but possibly another type of fir tree) and known to reach lenghts of up to 6 m, are attested in both pre-Sargonic and Old Babylonian sources (see Van de Mieroop 1992: 160, Powell 1992: 117–118 and Englund 2010).
8: this personal name is attested in Nippur (cf. Goddeeris 2016, nos. 10: 36 and 101: 37).
10: unfortunately, the amount charged for the rental of the boat here is lost. It could depend largely on what was being transported. As for the Ur III period, it has been suggested that a regular formula existed for figuring boat rental which factored in capacity and length of journey: 1 *sila* (= 1 litre) of barley per loaded *gur* (= 300 litres) per *danna* (one double-hour, i.e. the distance travelled in two hours).[41] According to the Laws of Ešnunna, the hire of a boat was 2 *sila* of barley per *gur* per day, whereas the Code of Hammurapi fixed the daily hire of a 60 *gur* capacity boat at $^1/_6$ shekel of silver (which at the "normal" price of barley, i.e. 1 *gur* of barley = 1 shekel of silver, works out to $^5/_6$ *sila* of barley per *gur* per day). For a list of some rental costs in the Old Babylonian contracts see Stol 1993–1995: 168b.
16–17: one of the main distinguishing features of model contracts is the omission of the list of witnesses and the date, both essential for the legal validity of functional contracts.[42] Some model contracts, including the contract here presented, allude to the witnesses and date that have been omitted by the notation "its witnesses, its month, its year".

§11 (C.ii. 5–28) Rental of a boat

C.ii.	5.	**1.**	1 ^{ĝeš}ma$_2$ 5(u)-⌜gur$^!$⌝
	6.	**2.**	1 ^{ĝeš}zi-⌜gan⌝
	7.	**3.**	3 ^{ĝeš}gi-muš
	8.	**4.**	4 ^{ĝeš}ĝisal
	9.	**5.**	2 eš$_2$ ma$_2$-gid$_2$-da
	10.	**6.**	^{ĝeš}ma$_2$ / ^{d}nanna-me-ša$_4$
	11.	**7.**	ki ^{d}nanna-me-ša$_4$-ta
	12.	**8.**	^{I}ur-^{d}šul-/pa-e$_3$-ke$_4$
	13.	**9.**	in-huĝ
	14.	**10.**	iti 2-am$_3$
	15.	**11.**	6$^?$(aš) ⌜še⌝ gur
	16.	**12.**	iti ⌜4$^?$⌝-am$_3$
	17.	**13.**	6$^?$(aš) še gur
	18.	**14.**	⌜šu⌝-niĝin 3$^?$(u)+[6$^?$(aš)] še gur
	19.	**15.**	^{I}ur-⌜^{d}⌝šul-/pa-[e$_3$]-ke$_4$
	20.	**16.**	^{I}⌜^{d}⌝[nanna-me-ša$_4$-r]a
	21.	**17.**	al-[aĝ$_2$-e]
	22.	**18.**	iti du$_6$-[kug-ka]
	23.	**19.**	^{ĝeš}m[a$_2$ silim-m]a
	24.	**20.**	u$_3$ ⌜a$_2$-bi⌝-še$_3$
	25.	**21.**	kar-bi-še$_3$
	26.	**22.**	gur-ru-dam
	27.	**23.**	lu$_2$-ki-inim-ma
	28.	**24.**	iti-bi mu-bi

41 Michalowski 1977: 292f: 1 ma$_2$ 20 gur da-na 1 gur 1 sila$_3$-ta. A slightly higher rate (1 $^1/_5$ *sila* per *gur* per double-hour) is attested in AUCT 1, 386. Cf. Englund 1988: 167–168 fn 40.
42 See Hallo 1975: 195–196.

"[7–9]Ur-Šulpa'e has rented from Nanna-meša [1–5]one boat of 50 *gur* capacity, one rudder, three punting poles, four oars, two ropes for towing the boat: [6](this is) the boat of Nanna-meša. [15–17]Ur-Šulpa'e [will pa]y (lit: will measure) t[o Nanna-meša] [11]6$^{?}$ *gur* of barley [10]for two months (and) [13]6$^{?}$ *gur* of barley [12] for four$^{?}$ months: [14]total 3[6$^{?}$] *gur* of barley. [18–22]The boat must be returned [in good condition], together with its rent, at its quay [in the se]venth month. [23–24](Its) witnesses, its month its year".

Notes

This rental contract is similar to the model contract quoted in Civil 1974–1977: 69–70 fn. 8: 3N-T567, a Type II tablet.[43]

4: the Sumerian term ^{ĝeš}ĝisal, equated to the Akkadian *gišallu* (OB Nippur Ura 1: 645) means "oar".

10–14: unfortunately, the surface of the prism is abraded and it is not easy to read the number of *gur* at lines 11 and 13, and in the total at line 14. I have tentatively read 6 *gur* on the basis of the parallel text, 3N-T567 o.i. 1–20, in which the formula a$_{2}$-bi iti-da 6(aš) še gur appears at lines 11–12. Considering a rental of 6 *gur* per month, the total during 6 months (2+4) would be 36 *gur*. Moreover, it is not clear why the scribe added another four months to the rental of the boat, which is lacking in the duplicate.

Duplicate:

3N-T567 (o.i. 1–20)[44]

o.i.	1.	**1.**	[1] ^{ĝeš}[ma$_{2}$ 5(u)-gur]
	2.	**2.**	[1] ^{ĝeš}zi-⸢gan⸣
	3.	**3.**	[3] ^{ĝeš}gi-muš
	4.	**4.**	⸢4⸣ ^{ĝeš}gisal
	5.	**5.**	[2] eš$_{2}^{!}$(TUG$_{2}$) <<SI>> ma$_{2}$-gid$_{2}$-da
	6.	**6.**	⸢^{ĝeš}⸣ma$_{2}$ ^{d}nanna-me-ša$_{4}$
	7.	**7.**	[k]i ^{d}nanna-me-ša$_{4}$-ta
	8.	**8.**	[^{I}u]r-^{d}šul-pa-e$_{3}^{!}$-ke$_{4}$
	9.	**9.**	⸢iti⸣ 2-kam-ma-še$_{3}$
	10.	**10.**	in-huĝ
	11.	**11.**	a$_{2}$-bi iti-da
	12.	**12.**	6(aš) še gur
	13.	**13.**	^{I}ur-^{d}šul-pa-e$_{3}$
	14.	**14.**	^{Id}nanna-me-ša$_{4}$-ra
	15.	**15.**	al-aĝ$_{2}$-e
	16.	**16.**	iti du$_{6}$-kug
	17.	**17.**	⸢^{ĝeš}⸣ma$_{2}$ silim-ma
	18.	**18.**	u$_{3}$ a$_{2}$-bi-še$_{3}$
	19.	**19.**	[ka]r nibru^{ki}-ta$^{\text{(sic)}}$
	20.	**20.**	[gur-r]u-dam

[43] Since this tablet is housed in the Iraq Museum, it was not possible to make collations of it; the transliteration offered below is based on the one made by Civil (some missing signs have been integrated on the basis of the HS text).

[44] Since Civil reports that this model contract was recorded on a Type II/1 tablet, it means that it was very likely written on the left column, that of the teacher.

"$^{7–10}$[U]r-Šulpa'e has rented from Nanna-meša for two months $^{1–5}$[one boat of 50 *gur* capacity, one] rudder, [three] punting poles, four oars, [two] ropes for towing the boat: ^{6}(this is) the boat of Nanna-meša. $^{13–15}$Ur-Šulpa'e will pay to Nanna-meša $^{11–12}$6 *gur* of barley as its monthly rent. $^{16–20}$The boat must b[e returned] in good condition, together with its rent, at$^{!}$ [the quay] of Nippur in the seventh month".

§12 (C.ii. 29–iii. 22) Hire of a slave

C.ii.	29.	**1.**	1 saĝ-nita$_2$
	30.	**2.**	^{I}ir$_{11}$-*iš$_8$-tar$_2$*
	31.	**3.**	mu-ni-im
	32.	**4.**	arad$_2$ *e-ri-ib*-AN
	33.	**5.**	ki *e-ri-ib*-⸢AN⸣-t[a]
C.iii.			*ca. 10 lines missing*
	11.	**16.**	EŠ$_2$ ⸢A$^?$/2$^?$ AB$^?$ NA⸣
	12.	**17.**	^{I}*ip-qu$_2$-ša*
	13.	**18.**	ninda an-ni-ib-/gu$_7$-e
	14.	**19.**	^{I}*e-ri-ib*-AN
	15.	**20.**	lugal-a-ni
	16.	**21.**	tug$_2$ an-ni-ib$_2$-/mu$_4$-mu$_4$
	17.	**22.**	tukum-bi
	18.	**23.**	arad$_2$-da-a-bi
	19.	**24.**	ba-uš$_2$ / ba-za[ḫ$_2$]
	20.	**25.**	u$_2$-gu ba-an-d[e$_2$]
	21.	**26.**	u$_3$ tu-ra / ba-an-⸢tu⸣
	22.	**27.**	⸢a$_2$$^?$⸣-ni-/še$_3$ ⸢a-ra$_2$ 2⸣-[kam]

"$^{1–4}$A man, named Warad-Ištar, the slave of Erīb-ilum, ^{5}from Erīb-ilum ... ^{16}... $^{17–18}$Ipquša will provide him with food $^{19–21}$(whereas) Erīb-ilum, his master, will provide him with clothing. $^{22–26}$If that slave dies, flees, disappears or falls ill, ^{27}for his work a second time (he, i.e. Erīb-ilum, will give to Ipquša a second slave)".

Notes

This incomplete contract likely records the hire of a slave owned by a certain Erīb-ilum by Ipquša (who appears at line 17 after a gap of ca. 10 lines). At the end of the contract there is the warranty against flight,[45] which often appears in the pledge contracts and in the hires of workers together with the warranty against delinquency.

18 and **21**: cf. Ai VI iii 18: lu$_2$-ḫuĝ-ĝa$_2$-a-ni ninda i$_3$-gu$_7$-e tug$_2$ am$_3$-mu$_4$-mu$_4$ / *a-gi-ir-*⸢*šu*⸣ *a-ka-lam u$_2$-ša$_2$-*⸢*kal*⸣ *u$_3$ ṣu-ba-ta u$_2$-lab-ba-*[*aš*], "he will provide his hireling with food and clothing".

24–26: the warranty against flight refers to the master's responsibility for a runaway slave: cf. FLP 1287 viii. 3–8 (= Roth 1979: 48);[46] cf. also Ai VII iv 13–22 and Ura 1 364–369.

---

[45] To prevent a slave from running away, physical impediments such as chains and fetters were available. The law punished persons who aided or harbored fugitive slaves and offered a reward for their return.

[46] [t]ukum-⸢bi⸣ / [ba-uš$_2$] / [ba-an]-zaḫ$_2$-a / ⸢u$_2$⸣-gu ba-an-de$_2$ / u$_3$ tu-ra / ba-an-tu / a$_2$-ĝeš-ĝar-ra-ni-še$_3$ / bi$_2$-ib-si-si-ge, "if [(the slave-girl) dies, fl]ees, disappears or falls ill, he (= the debtor) will pay in full for her assigned work.

25: as Steinkeller has noted (1989: 69–70), in lexical texts the Sumerian verb ugu ~ de$_2$ is equated primarily with Akkadian *nābutu*, "to run away, to flee" (cf. CAD A$_1$, *s.v. abātu*, 2, p. 45f.) and secondarily with *ḫalāqu*, "to disappear, to vanish, to become missing or lost, to escape" (cf. CAD Ḫ, *s.v. ḫalāqu*, p. 37). The lexical tradition considered *nābutu* to be the main equivalent of ugu ~ de$_2$ (cf. Ai VII iv 16–17 and Ura 1 364–365), whereas *ḫalāqu* is given as the translation of zaḫ$_{2/3}$. However, Steinkeller has remarked that in III millennium texts the meaning "to escape" is expressed by zaḫ$_{2/3}$ and not by ugu ~ de$_2$, which seems to mean "to vanish, to get lost", since it is said almost exclusively of objects and animals. He therefore concludes that, contrary to the lexical tradition, the original equivalent of ugu ~ de$_2$ was *ḫalāqu* and not *nābutu*.
26: here the Sumerian expression tu-ra ba-an-tu (or tu-ra ba-ab-ak, cf. Ai. VII iv 19), equated to the Akkadian verb *marāṣu*, does not refer to a short-term disease, but to a lenghty one preventing the hired man from performing work. In two cautionary clauses in labour contracts (UET 5 204 r. 2 and BM 97571 r. 1, from Ur and Sippar respectively), instead, the Akkadian verb to express a chronic illness is *salāḫu* (see Stol 2009: 32).
27: this elliptical formula is not known to me from other texts; the integration and translation, which are to be considered merely tentative, are based on the context. After the warranty against flight, one expects a clause regarding the penalty to be paid by the owner of the slave.

§13 (C.iii. 23–D.i. 18) Content not completely identified (slave)

C.iii.	23.	**1.**	1 saĝ-⸢nita$_2$⸣
	24.	**2.**	^{I}⸢*šu*$^?$⸣-*i*$_3$$^?$-*li*$_2$$^?$-⸢*šu*⸣
	25.	**3.**	mu-ni-i[m]
	26.	**4.**	lu$_2$-en-nu-/uĝ$_3$-⸢ĝa$_2$⸣
	27.	**5.**	abul-la-ta
	28.	**6.**	nu-um-ta-⸢e$_3$⸣(⸢UD⸣.[DU])
	29.	**7.**	arad$_2$-⸢da⸣-[a-bi]
	30.	**8.**	ki l[u$_2$-en-nu-uĝ$_3$-ta$^?$]
	31.	**9.**	⸢in⸣-[...]
D.i.			*ca. 2 lines missing*
			traces of 5 lines
	8$^?$.	**17.**	⸢x⸣-[...]-⸢še$_3$⸣ / i[n]-⸢x⸣
	9.	**18.**	tug$_2$ an-⸢ni⸣-⸢ib$_2$⸣-/mu$_4$-⸢mu$_4$⸣
	10.	**19.**	tuku/m-bi (ŠU.ĜAR.TUR/LAL.BI)
	11.	**20.**	arad$_2$-da-a-ni
	12.	**21.**	u$_2$-gu ba/-an-⸢de$_2$⸣
	13.	**22.**	$^1/_3$$^?$ ma-⸢na kug-babbar⸣
	14.	**23.**	^{I}*a*-⸢*ḫa*$^?$⸣-/*nir*-⸢*ši*-ke$_4$⸣
	15.	**24.**	⸢lu$_2$-na$^?$-me$^?$⸣ / in-na-⸢pad$_3$⸣
	16.	**25.**	i$_3$-la$_2$-⸢e⸣
	17.	**26.**	lu$_2$-ki-inim-ma
	18.	**27.**	[it]i-⸢bi⸣ mu-bi

"$^{4–6}$The one (in charge) of the guard did not let out from the gate $^{1–3}$a man, named Šu-ilīšu$^?$; $^{7–9}$[that$^?$] slave from the one [(in charge) of the guard$^?$ ...]; [...] ^{17}... ^{18}he will provide him with clothing. $^{19–21}$If his slave disappears, ^{23}Aḫam-nirši (= the master of the slave) ^{25}will pay (lit: will weigh) ^{22}20$^?$ shekels of silver ^{24}to anyone who finds the slave for him (= Aḫam-nirši). $^{26–27}$(Its) witnesses, its m[onth], its year".

Notes

Unfortunately, due to the large lacuna in the text, it is not entirely clear what is happening here. In the first part we know that the guard did not allow Šu-ilīšu$^?$, who is a slave (l. 7), to get out from the city gate. Then, after a certain number of missing lines, it is said that someone will provide the slave with clothing. Finally, it is said that, in case of the slave's disappearance, Aḫam-nirši, the owner of the slave (who, in fact is defined as "his slave" at line 20; see also comm. at l. 23 below), will pay a reward of 20 shekels to anyone who finds his slave. Because of the gaps and the damages to the surface, however, this proposal is only tentative.

5–6: a similar situation occurs in another unpublished model contract from Nippur (cf. N 6005 o.i. 4–5, P230694).

22–25: a comparable case is recorded in the Laws of Ur-Namma (§16), where it is said that "if ... a female slave escapes and crosses the township limits, and someone brings her back, the owner of the slave will pay 2 shekels of silver to the man who brought her back" (cf. Civil 2011: 247).[47] The very same reward of 2 shekels is also found in the Hammurapi Code §17: "if a man seizes a fugitive slave or slave woman in the open country and leads him back to his owner the slave owner shall give him 2 shekels of silver" (cf. Roth 1995: 84).[48]

23: a similar personal name, Aḫam-arši, "I have obtained a brother", is the Akkadian reading of the Sumerian šeš-ba-an-tuku, as it occurs in the text MRAH O.120 (= Limet 2000: 16). At its upper edge, in fact, we find the notation ⸢*a*⸣*-ḫa-am-mar-ši*, which is the Akkadian translation of that Sumerian name (cf. Roth 1979: 109 and 148 n. 15). šeš-ba-an-tuku can be considered a "school name", often used as the owner of a slave (for the list of the model contracts mentioning him see Bodine 2015: 173–175 and the additions in Spada 2017b: 293). I wonder whether the name Aḫam-nirši, "We have obtained a brother" could also be considered a variant reading of that Sumerian personal name and, therefore a school name.

In the lower part of the first column and in the preserved part of the second one there are not more than 21/22 visible lines (many of them seem to be indented). Unfortunately, the few readable signs do not allow us to figure out if they belong to just one or more contracts and to understand its (or their) content.

§14 (D.i. 19–23)

D.i.	19.	**1.**	[...] ⸢x x⸣
	20.	**2.**	[x] ⸢x⸣ ḪAR / [(x)] ⸢x 5$^?$⸣
	21.	**3.**	[...] ⸢x⸣ SI ⸢KI$^?$⸣
	22.	**4.**	[...] ⸢x⸣ US$_2$$^?$/GIM$^?$
	23.	**5.**	[...] ⸢ta$^?$⸣

§15$^?$ (D.ii. 1'–21')

D.ii.			*traces of 7 lines with scattered signs*
	8'	**1'.**	1 ⸢x x⸣ [...]
	9'	**2'.**	^{I}a-[...] / ⸢x⸣
	10'	**3'.**	⸢x⸣-[...]-/a-ni
	11'.	**4'.**	*erasure*
	12'.	**5'.**	1 ⸢saĝ$^?$ x⸣ [...]

[47] tu[kum-bi] ⸢x⸣ [...]-⸢a$^?$⸣ geme$_2$ ba-[za]ḫ$_3$ ki-sur-ra ⸢ere⸣-na-ka ib$_2$-te-bal lu$_2$ ⸢im⸣-mi-gur [lu]gal saĝ-ĝa$_2$-ke$_4$ lu$_2$ im-mi-in-gur-ra 2 giĝ$_4$ kug-babbar i$_3$-(n[a])-la$_2$-e.

[48] *šumma awīlum lu wardam lu amtam ḫalqam ina ṣērim iṣbatma ana bēlišu irtediaššu* 2 *šiqil kaspam bēl wardim inaddiššum.*

13’ **6’.** ⸢x⸣ [...]
14’ **7’.** ⸢x⸣ [...]
15’. **8’.** e$_2^?$-⸢x⸣ [inim] / ⸢nu$^?$⸣-um$^?$-ĝ[a$_2^?$-ĝa$_2^?$-a$^?$]
16’. **9’.** tuk[um-bi](ŠU.ĜAR.TU[R.LAL.BI])
17’. **10’.** dumu$^?$ [...] / ⸢⸢x x⸣ [...]
18’. **11’.** ⸢x⸣ [...] / ⸢x x x⸣
19’. **12’.** kug$^?$ ⸢x⸣ / ⸢x la$^?$-ta$^?$⸣
20’ **13’.** e$_2^?$ ⸢x x⸣
21’. **14’.** ba-⸢an⸣-ši-⸢x-x⸣
rest broken

2

Museum n°: HS 1851
Plates: 5 and 21
Measurements: 6×4.9×3 cm
State of preservation: the prism is very fragmentary, and just two of the original four sides are preserved.

It is not possible to infer the exact number of columns per side, since just two columns and one column are preserved in side A and side B respectively; however, presumably, there were three or four in origin, as usual
All the model contracts, partially preserved, record loan contracts.

Inner organization of the prism:

	Side A	
§1	loan of unknown commodity	i'. 1'–10'
§2	barley loan	ii'. 1'–2'
§3	barley loan	ii'. 3'–10'

	Side B	
§4	partnership loan	i. 1'–3'
§5	partnership agreement	i. 4'–6'

§1 (A.i'. 1'–10') Loan of unknown commodity

A.i'.		*unknown number of lines missing*
1'.	**1'.**	[gur]-ru-de$_3$
2'.	**2'.**	[...-g]i$_4^?$-eš
3'.	**3'.**	[tuk]um-bi ([ŠU.ĜAR.TUR].LAL.BI)
4'.	**4'.**	[...]-ka
5'.	**5'.**	[gur]-ru-de$_3$
6'.	**6'.**	[...]-⸢gi$_4$⸣-eš
7'.	**7'.**	[...]-⸢x⸣-nam$^?$
8'.	**8'.**	[...]-⸢x⸣-bi
9'.	**9'.**	[...]-NE
10'.	**10'.**	[...]-⸢x⸣

Notes
Unfortunately, in the first column just the final signs are preserved and it is not possible to reconstruct correctly the missing parts, although the preserved formulas are clearly related to a loan contract.

§2 (A.ii'. 1'–2') Partnership$^{?}$ loan

A.ii'. *unknown number of lines missing*

1'. **1'.** la-ba-an-su$_{8}$-g[e-eš]

2'. **2'.** še ⸢x x$^{?}$⸣ ba-[ra$^{?}$]-/ab-šum$_{2}$-m[u-ne]

"... [if $^{1'}$they] have not gone (on a business trip to ...), $^{2'}$they will give the barley ...".

Notes

Unfortunately only the final part of this loan contract is preserved, and it is not possible to fully understand what it records. However, the verbal expression in l. 1' seems to suggest that it is the final part of a partnership loan. This type of loan is relatively common among model contracts (cf. OBMC catalogue). Usually, one or more persons borrow silver from an investor (the creditor, Sumerian um-mi-a) for partnership in a commercial venture. When the commercial transactions are completed, the investor is repaid and the partners divide profits and share losses.[49] For this type of loan contract see also the commentary to **4** §7, §§10–12 and §14.

1': the same verbal form appears in a badly damaged tablet, CBS 2298, which contains a model contract recording a partnership loan.[50]

2': the two (or three) signs which follow še are not readable and do not seem to match with any expression typical of loan contracts.

CBS 2298 (o. 1–15)

o. **1.** *one line missing*
2. maš$_{2}$ ⸢nu-ub-tuku⸣
3. kaš sa$_{10}$-sa$_{10}$-⸢de$_{3}$⸣
4. ki ^{d}nin$^{?}$-urta-ta
5. ^{I}lu$_{2}$-gid$_{2}$-gid$_{2}$
6. ^{I}ur-^{d}EN.ZU
7. u$_{3}$ *a-gu*-⸢*u*$_{2}$$^{?}$⸣-[*a*$^{?}$-ke$_{4}$$^{?}$]
8. šu ba-an-⸢ti⸣-eš
9. ⸢ud buru$_{14}$-a⸣-ka
10. kaš sa$_{10}$-sa$_{10}$-d[e$_{3}$]
11. al-su$_{8}$-ge-[ne$^{?}$]
12. tukum-[bi]
13. kaš sa$_{10}$-sa$_{10}$-d[e$_{3}$]
14. la-ba-an-su$_{8}$-ge-e[š]
15. [x-b]i al-gi-i[n-x]
rest broken

"$^{5-8}$Lu-gidgid, Ur-Sîn and Agū'a have received ^{4}from Ninurta $^{1-3}$(tot. *gur* of barley), without interest, for buying beer; $^{9-11}$at harvest time they will go (on a business trip) to buy beer. $^{12-15}$If they have not gone (on a business trip) to buy beer, its [...] ...".

---

[49] For a comprehensive study on the partnership loans see Dole 1965. Cf. also Eilers 1931: 5–37, Lautner 1939: 24–79 and Szlechter 1947.

[50] I thank Ricardo Dorado Puntch for having brought it to my attention and for providing me a tentative transliteration and translation of the text.

§3 (A.ii'. 3'–10') Barley loan

A.ii'.	3'.	**1.**	3(aš) š[e gur]
	4'.	**2.**	mu šeš-a-n[i]
	5'.	**3.**	maš$_2$ nu-mu-ni-⸢in⸣-tu[ku]
	6'.	**4.**	ki ^{d}EN.ZU-*i-din-na*[*m*]
	7'.	**5.**	^{I}šeš-du$_{10}$-ga-⸢ke$_4$⸣
	8'.	**6.**	šu ba-an-ti
	9'.	**7.**	iti kin-^{d}inana
	10'.	**8.**	še al-aĝ$_2$-e

"$^{5-6}$Šeš-duga, has received ^{4}from Sîn-iddina[m] $^{1-2}$3 [*gur* of barl]ey in his brother's name – ^{3}the interest has not been charged to it. $^{7-8}$He will measure the barley in the sixth month".

Notes

2–3: a similar phrase is also attested in an unpublished model contract recording a barley loan (CBS 6542 o.i. 1'–10', P229216), but instead of "brother" the term "comrade" (gu$_5$-li) appears: mu gu$_5$-li-⸢a⸣-ni maš$_2$ nu-mu-ni-tuku (ll. 2'–3'). The very same expression, mu gu$_5$-li-a-ni, occurs also in another model contract (CBS 10311 r.i'. 3'–7', P230794), however without the following verbal form.

3: the reason for the scribe's use of this verbal form rather than the usual "nu-(ub)-tuku" is not entirely clear to me.

§4 (B.i. 1'–3') Partnership loan

B.i.			*unknown number of lines missing and traces*
	1'.	**1'.**	[mi]n$_3$-⸢na⸣-[ne-ne]
	2'.	**2'.**	teš$_2$-a si$_3$-[ga-bi]
	3'.	**3'.**	i$_3$-ba-[e-ne]

"...$^{1'}$the two of them $^{3'}$will div[ide] $^{2'}$equally among themselves".

§5 (B.i. 4'–6') Partnership agreement

B.i.	4'.	**1.**	1(u) 2(aš) [še gur]
	5'.	**2.**	sig$_9$-ga ^{d}na[nna-x]
	6'.	**3.**	5(aš) ur$^{?}$-šu-bu$^{?}$-l[a$^{?}$]

"^{1}12 [*gur* of barley], ^{2}(is) the investment share of Na[nna-x], ^{3}5 (*gur* of barley, is the investment share of) Ur-Šubul[a$^{?}$] ...".

Notes

2: the presence of the Sumerian term sig$_9$-ga, "investment share"(equated to the Akkadian *šipkātu*; cf. CAD Š$_3$, *s.v. šipkātu*, mng. 2b, p. 70), identifies this text as one dealing with a commercial partnership. However, since only the first three lines have been preserved, it is not possible to determine whether it records the formation of a partnership, the dissolution of it or another type of transaction. For the dissolution of a partnership cf. **4** §14.

3.

Museum n°: HS 2607
Plates: 5 and 21
Measurements: 6.4×5×4.9 cm.
State of preservation: this prism is very fragmentary, and only two of the original four sides are preserved.

Each side has two partial columns (presumably they were three or four in origin); in this preserved portion of the prism, we can identify five model contracts.

Inner organization of the prism:

	Side A	
§1	rental for storing barley	i’. 1’–6’
§2	barley loan	ii’. 1’–10’
§3	barley loan	ii’. 11’–12’

	Side B	
§4	content not completely identified	i’. 1’–10’
§5	barley loan	ii’. 1’–9’

§1 (A.i’. 1’–6’) Rental for storing barley

A.i’.		*unknown number of lines missing*
1’.	**1’.**	[i$_3$-la$_2$]-⸢e$^?$⸣
2’.	**2’.**	[šag$_4^?$ zu$_2$]-keš$_2$-bi-<ta>
3’.	**3’.**	[x giĝ$_4$ k]ug-babbar
4’.	**4’.**	[^{I}*i$_3$-li$_2$-am-r*]*a*-⸢*an*⸣-*ni*
5’.	**5’.**	[šu ba-an-t]i
6’.	**6’.**	[ib$_2$-tak$_4$ z]u$_2$-keš$_2$-/[b]i
		rest of column missing

“(Lu-Ninurta$^?$) $^{1'}$will$^?$ [pay] (to Ilī-amranni x shekel(s) of silver a year). $^{2'}$[From] this re[nt $^{4'–5'}$Ilī-amr]anni has re[ceived $^{3'}$x shekel(s) of s]ilver. (Lu-Ninurta will weigh) $^{6'}$[the rest of the re]nt [in the ... month]”.

Notes
This badly preserved contract is tentatively identified as the rental of a real estate[51] and restored on the basis of two duplicates from Nippur contained in two Type II tablets: CBS 8663+ and Ist Ni 1576. Other similar texts appear in two multi-column tablets: MS 3176/5 (the provenience of which is unknown)[52] and UM 55-21-441 (from Nippur).

[51] For the problems that could arise when a man stored his grain in somebody else’s house cf. Civil 2011: 268–270.
[52] Cf. Civil 2011: 268–269, where a transliteration of this model contract appears. See also fn. 58 below.

Duplicates:

CBS 8663+ (o.i. 1'–r.i'. 4)[53]

o.i.	1'.	**1.**	4$^{?}$(u) [še gur]
	2'.	**2.**	e$_2$ UŠ.UŠ ⸢x⸣ [...]
	3'.	**3.**	^{I}*i*$_3$-*li*$_2$-*am-ra-an-n*[*i*]
	4'.	**4.**	^{I}lu$_2$-^{d}nin-ur[ta]
	5'.	**5.**	in-s[ig$_9$]
	6'.	**6.**	a$_2$-bi [iti-da]
	7'.	**7.**	⸢2$^{?}$(u) še⸣ k[ug-babbar-ta-am$_3$]
	8'.	**8.**	⸢mu⸣-[am$_3$ 1 $^{1}/_{3}$ giĝ$_4$ kug-babbar]
	9'.	**9.**	[^{I}lu$_2$]-⸢^{d}nin-urta⸣-[ke$_4$]
	10'.	**10.**	^{I}*i*$_3$-*li*$_2$-*am-ra-an-ni*-ra
	11'.	**11.**	i$_3$-la$_2$-e
	12'.	**12.**	šag$_4$ zu$_2$-keš$_2$-bi-ta
	13'.	**13.**	⸢$^{2}/_{3}$ giĝ$_4$⸣ kug-babbar
	14'.	**14.**	⸢*i*$_3$-*li*$_2$⸣-*am-ra-an-ni*-ke$_4$
	15'.	**15.**	šu ba-an-ti
	16'.	**16.**	ib$_2$-tak$_4$ zu$_2$-keš$_2$-bi
	17'.	**17.**	iti ud$_2^{duru5}$-ka i$_3$-la$_2$-e
	18'.	**18.**	[tu]ku[m]-bi
	19'.	**19.**	[e$_2$-b]i al-burud$_x$(U)
	20'.	**20.**	[u$_3$ kišib-bi] al-ze$_2$-er
r.i'.	1.	**21.**	[še] niĝ$_2$ u$_2$-gu ba-[an-de$_2$]
	2.	**22.**	[^{I}*i*$_3$]-*li*$_2$-*am-ra-an-ni* ⸢lugal⸣ [e$_2$-a]
	3.	**23.**	[^{I}]lu$_2$-^{d}nin-urta-ra
	4.	**24.**	[b]i$_2^{?}$-ib-si-si

"$^{4-5}$Lu-Ninur[ta has deposited for sto]rage $^{1-3}$40$^{?}$ [*gur* of barley] in the house ... of Ilī-amrann[i]; $^{6-7}$the [monthly] rent (for this deposit) is 20 grains of sil[ver]. $^{9-11}$[Lu]-Ninurta will pay to Ilī-amranni ^{8}[1 $^{1}/_{3}$ shekels of silver per] year. $^{12-15}$From this rent Ilī-amranni has received $^{2}/_{3}$ shekels of silver. $^{16-17}$He (= Lu-Ninurta) will pay the rest of the rent in the eleventh month. $^{18-20}$If th[at house] is burglarized [and that sealed tablet[54]] is broken (i.e. the document is invalidated), $^{22-24}$[I]lī-amranni, the owner [of the house], will repay to Lu-Ninurta ^{21}[the barley] that has been lost".

Ist Ni 1576 (o.i. 1'–10')

o.i.			[...]
	1'.	**1'.**	[^{I}lu$_2$-^{d}nin-urta]
	2'.	**2'.**	[i]n-sig$_9$
	3'.	**3'.**	[a$_2$]-bi iti-da
	4'.	**4'.**	[2(u)] še kug-babbar-ta-am$_3$
	5'.	**5'.**	[m]u-am$_3$ 1 $^{1}/_{3}$ giĝ$_4$ kug-babbar
	6'.	**6'.**	[^{I}]lu$_2$-^{d}nin-urta-ke$_4$
	7'.	**7'.**	*i*$_3$-*li*$_2$-*am-ra-ni*-ra

[53] For the reader's sake, also its complete translation is provided.

[54] Here the term kišib could also refer to the clay sealing on the locked door of the storage-room which has been burglarized (Stol, personal communication, October 2017).

8’. **8’.** i$_3$-la$_2$-e
9’. **9’.** šag$_4$ zu$_2$-keš$_2$-bi-t[a]
10’. **10’.** $^2/_3$ giĝ$_4$ ku[g-babbar]
rest of column missing

MS 3176/5 (r.i. 17–34)

r.i. 17. **1.** 1(u) še gur
18. **2.** e$_2$ *i$_3$-li$_2$-am-ra-ni*
19. **3.** ^{I}lu$_2$-^{d}nin-šubur
20. **4.** in-sig$_9$-ge
21. **5.** a$_2$-bi iti-da
22. **6.** $^1/_3$ giĝ$_4$-ta-am$_3$
23. **7.** mu-am$_3$ 4 giĝ$_4$ kug-babbar
24. **8.** ^{I}lu$_2$-^{d}nin-šubur
25. **9.** ^{I}*i$_3$-li$_2$-am-ra-ni*-ra
26. **10.** i$_3$-la$_2$-e
27. **11.** tukum-bi
28. **12.** e$_2$-bi al-burud$_x$
29. **13.** u$_3$ kišib-bi al-ze-er
30. **14.** še niĝ$_2$ u$_2$-gu ba-an-de$_2$
31. **15.** ^{I}*i$_3$-li$_2$-am-ra-ni*
32. **16.** lugal e$_2$-a
33. **17.** še bi$_2$-ib-si-si
34. **18.** mu lugal-la-bi in-pad$_3$

UM 55-21-441 (r.ii. 1’–3’)

r.ii. *upper part of the column destroyed*
1’. **1’.** [^{I}*i$_3$-li$_2$*]-⸢*am-ra-an*⸣-*ni*-e
2’. **2’.** ^{I}lu$_2$-^{d}nin-urta-ra
3’. **3’.** bi$_2$-ib-si-si

§2 (A.ii’. 1’–10’) Barley loan

A.ii’. *ca. 4 lines missing*
1’. **1’.** [šu]-⸢ba-an⸣-[ti]
2’. **2’.** [it]i ⸢šeg$_{12}$-a⸣-[ka]
3’. **3’.** [k]ar n[ibru^{ki}(E[N.LIL$_2$.KI])-ka]
4’. **4’.** [a]l-a[ĝ$_2$-e]
5’. **5’.** tuku[m-bi] (ŠU.ĜAR.TUR.[LAL.BI])
6’. **6’.** iti šeg$_{12}$-⸢a⸣-[ka]
7’. **7’.** kar ni[bru^{ki}(EN.[LIL$_2$.KI])-ka]
8’. **8’.** la-ba-a[ĝ$_2$-e]
9’. **9’.** maš$_2$ 1(aš) gur [1(barig) 4(ban$_2$) še-ta-am$_3$]
10’. **10’.** bi$_2$-i[b-taḫ-e]

"[PN$_2$ $^{1'}$has rec]eived [x *gur* of barley, without interest, from PN$_1$]; $^{2'–4'}$[he will mea]sure it [in] the third month [at the q]uay of N[ippur]; $^{5'–8'}$i[f in the] third month he will not me[asure it at the] quay of Ni[ppur], $^{9'–10'}$he [will add] an interest of [1 *bariga* 4 *ban* (= 100 *sila*) of barley per] 1 *gur*".

Notes

3': as Skaist notes, in many loan contracts there is a clause saying that the loan is to be repaid at a certain place, and the place most frequently mentioned is the quay (Sumerian kar, Akkadian *kārum*) of a town (cf. Skaist 1994: 190–191).

§3 (A.ii'. 11'–12') Barley loan

A.ii'.	11'.	**1.**	5$^?$(u) ⸢še⸣ [gur]
	12'.	**2.**	⸢maš$_2$⸣ [...]
			broken

"^{1}50$^?$ [*gur* of] barley, ^{2}(its) interest...".

§4 (B.i'. 1'–10')

B.i'.			*ca. five lines with scattered signs*
	6'.	**6'.**	[...] še$_3$
	7'.	**7'.**	[...] ⸢gaz$^?$⸣
	8'.	**8'.**	[...] ⸢x⸣ [x] še$_3$
	9'.	**9'.**	[...] ⸢x⸣ tak$_4^?$
	10'.	**10'.**	[...]-ni-še$_3$

Notes

Unfortunately this is a very damaged contract and only the final signs of some lines are preserved. These few signs, however, seem to recall some of the formulas appearing in a manumission contract (for this typology see the commentary to text **1** above). A tentative reconstruction of these lines could be: [dug nam-geme$_2$/arad-ni]-še$_3$ / [in]-⸢gaz$^?$⸣ / [kišib nam-sikil-l]a-[ni]-še$_3$ / [in-na]-⸢an$^?$⸣-tak$_4^?$ / [PN ud til$_3$-la]-ni-še$_3$ / [igi-ni-še$_3$ i$_3$-gub-bu].

§5 (B.ii'. 1'–9') Barley loan

B.ii'.	1'.	**1.**	[...] ⸢x⸣-[...]
	2'.	**2.**	[ki x]-šu-[...]
	3'.	**3.**	^{I}⸢x-x⸣-[...]
	4'.	**4.**	šu ba-[an-ti]
	5'.	**5.**	iti š[eg$_{12}$-a-ka]
	6'.	**6.**	1(aš) gur [še$^?$]
	7'.	**7.**	al-[aĝ$_2$-e]
	8'.	**8.**	lu$_2$-[ki-inim-ma]
	9'.	**9.**	[it]i$^?$-[bi mu-bi]

"$^{3–4'}$PN$_2$ has rece[ived x *gur* of barley] ^{2}[from PN$_1$]; $^{5–7}$[he will mea]sure 1 *gur* [of barley$^?$ in the th]ird month. $^{8–9}$[(Its) witn]esses, [its month, its year]".

2. Type I tablet

4.
Museum n°: HS 2500a[55]
Plates: 6–7 and 22–23
Measurements: 6.3×5.1×1.2 cm
State of preservation: upper half of the tablet.

This five-column tablet, because of its tiny size, can be labeled as a "micro-tablet".[56] Apart from its unusual size, it has all the features belonging to Type I tablets. These educational tools, which are large multi-column tablets (ca. 15×20 cm), ranging from two to six columns on each side and written in a relatively small script, usually contain an entire literary or lexical composition of several hundred lines, or a collection of model contracts. These tablets seem to contain exercises from the more advanced students, rather than standard reference copies.

The lower part of the obverse is broken; at the end of the last column of the reverse there is a colophon, with the name of the junior scribe (dub-sar tur), and his patronymic. It is followed by a box-design, filling the empty space in the column; finally, on the lower edge, there is a doxology to Nisaba, the goddess of writing.[57]

The preserved part of the tablet collects twenty model contracts, including several types of loans (barley loans, silver loans and partnership loans), sales of real estate and two house rentals.[58]

It is interesting to notice that there is an ascending progression in the quantities of barley or silver lent, which is visible in some of the preserved contract loans. In the first column of the obverse it starts with one *gur* of barley, followed by two *gur*; the loans of three and four *gur* are likely lost; then, in the second colum there is a loan of five *gur*. The very same situation can be observed among the silver loans: the first one, in the fourth column, is a loan of one shekel and, after a gap due to the break of the tablet, there is the loan of six shekels in the last column of the obverse. On the reverse, in the first column, the progression starts again with loans of one mina, two minas and three minas of silver.

---

[55] HS 2500b is a fragment of a micro-tablet (3×3×1.2 cm) with three columns on the obverse and four columns on the reverse, kept in the same box with HS 2500a. Although it seems to have been written by the same hand, it cannot be considered part of HS 2500a, since a more accurate analysis reveals that the columns in the fragment are narrower than those of our tablet.

[56] For a discussion about the making of a "micro-tablet" in antiquity see Sperl 1967.

[57] The colophon and the conventional invocation of Nisaba, ^{d}nisaba-za$_3$-mi$_2$ ('Nisaba be praised!') are typical of Type I tablets and Prisms.

[58] A very similar micro-tablet (MS 3176/5), collecting nineteen model contracts (including several types of loans, two legal cases about barley loans, and two house rentals for storing barley), will be published by the writer together with other model contracts housed in the Schøyen Collection.

Inner organization of the tablet:

	Obverse	
§1	barley loan	i. 1–10
§2	barley loan	i. 11–13
§3	barley loan	ii. 1–7
§4	barley loan	ii. 8–19
§5	barley loan	iii. 1–5
§6	barley loan	iii. 6–17
§7	partnership loan	iv. 1–9
§8	silver loan	iv. 10–16
§9	silver loan	v. 1–15

	Reverse	
§10	partnership loan	i. 1'–10'
§11	partnership loan	i. 11'–23'
§12	partnership loan	i. 24'–28'
§13	rental of a house for storing barley	ii. 1'–18'
§14	dissolution of a partnership	ii. 19'–29'
§15	rental of a house	ii. 30'–iii. 17'
§16	sale of a field	iii. 18'–28'
§17	sale of an orchard	iv. 1'–11'
§18	silver loan with a pledge	iv. 12'–24'
§19	silver loan	iv. 25'
§20	repayment of a silver loan	v. 1'–10'
	colophon	v. 11'–13'
	doxology	v. 14'

§ 1 (o.i. 1–10) Barley loan

o.i.	1.	**1.**	1(aš) še gur
	2.	**2.**	⸢maš$_2$ 1(aš) gur 1(barig) 4(ban$_2$) še⸣-ta-am$_3$
	3.	**3.**	⸢sig$_9$-ge$_4$⸣-de$_3$
	4.	**4.**	[ki x-x]-⸢x⸣-⸢ta⸣
	5.	**5.**	[^{I}...]-e
	6.	**6.**	[šu ba-an]-ti
	7.	**7.**	⸢iti šeg$_{12}$-a⸣-ka
	8.	**8.**	š[um$_2$]-⸢mu⸣-dam
	9.	**9.**	[lu$_2$]-ki-inim-ma
	10.	**10.**	⸢iti-bi⸣ mu-bi

"$^{5–6}$[PN$_2$ has recei]ved ^{4}from [PN$_1$] $^{1–3}$1 *gur* of barley – an interest rate of 1 *barig* 4 *ban* (= 100 *sila*) of barley per 1 *gur* is to be charged; $^{7–8}$to be g[iven (back)] in the third month. $^{9–10}$(Its) witnesses, its month, its year".

Notes

2–3: the interest rate clause is formulated here as a verbal sentence and corresponds to the standard interest rate of 33.3% (cf. Skaist 1994: 115–119). The verbal form sig$_9$-ge$_4$-de$_3$ appears frequently in the model contracts recording barley loans, as a verb of charging interest.[59]

7–8: for a description of the repayment clause and its components see Skaist 1994: 148–201. In particular, cf. p. 168 where the author states that the third month of the Nippur calendar (iti šeg$_{12}$-a) is the month most commonly used in the loan documents to indicate the term of the loan in the South, and specifically in Nippur loans.

§2 (o.i. 11–13) Barley loan

o.i. 11. **1.** ⌜2(aš) še gur⌝
12. **2.** ⌜maš$_2$⌝ [1(aš) gur] ⌜1(barig) 4(ban$_2$) še-ta-am$_3$⌝
13. **3.** [sig$_9$-ge$_4$]-⌜de$_3$⌝
traces of 3 lines
rest of column missing

"[PN$_2$ has received from PN$_1$] $^{1–3}$2 *gur* of barley, – [an interest rate] of 1 *barig* 4 *ban* (= 100 *sila*) of barley [per 1 *gur*] is to [be charged] ...".

§3 (o.ii. 1–7) Barley loan

the contract begins in the previous column
o.ii. 1. **1'.** un$^{?}$-dug$_3$
2. **2'.** kišib-bi ki ⌜*šu*-^{d}*adad*$^{?}$-ta⌝
3. **3'.** u$_2$-⌜gu ba⌝-[an]-⌜de$_2$⌝
4. **4'.** ⌜gaba-ri⌝ [kišib]-⌜ba⌝-ni
5. **5'.** [in]-⌜na-an-tak$_4$⌝
6. **6'.** ud [kur$_2$-še$_3$]
7. **7'.** kišib ⌜ul⌝-pa[d$_3$ zi-re]-⌜dam⌝

"... $^{1'}$after [PN$_1$ (= the debtor)] had satisfied [the heart of Šu-Adad], $^{2'–3'}$its (= of the repayment) sealed tablet has been lost from (the house of) Šu-Adad, (so that) $^{4'–5'}$he (= Šu-Adad) has drawn up for him a copy of his [sealed tablet]. $^{6'–7'}$In the [future], should the (lost) tablet be found, it has to be [destroyed]".

---

[59] See the edition of barley loans in OBMC. For the use of si.g "to add, charge (interest)" in interest clauses cf. Steinkeller 1981: 142 fn. 77; see also Widell 2002. For a different use of the verbal form sig$_9$-ge$_4$-de$_3$ see CUNES 52-10-147+ Side A i. 9', which records the exchange of real estates: sig$_9$-ge$_4$-de$_3$ seems to have the same meaning of the expression ki-be$_2$/ba ĝar/ĝa$_2$-ĝa$_2$, found in the Old Babylonian exchange documents from Nippur, meaning "to exchange". An edition of CUNES 52-10-147+ and of other model contracts housed in the Rosen Collection is in preparation by the writer.

Notes

Only the final part of this loan contract is preserved, containing the clause in the event of loss of the sealed tablet. We know that only one copy of a tablet recording a loan was drawn up and it was kept by the creditor:[60] if the tablet is lost (u$_2$-gu ~ de$_2$), it cannot be given back to the debtor in order to be broken, and a new tablet, a copy, must be drawn up (tak$_4$). However, if the old tablet is found (pad$_3$), it has to be destroyed immediately (zir). This same situation appears in numerous Ur III texts[61] and Old Babylonian model contracts,[62] including §9 in this same tablet.

1': this is the verbal part of the expression "the heart of PN/his heart is satisfied" (in Sumerian šag$_4$ ~ dug$_3$), one of the most widespread legal phrases in the ancient Near East (found frequently in Sumerian, Akkadian, Aramaic and Demotic), which has been thoroughly studied by Muffs 1968 and, more recently, by Westbrook 1991. In the Old Babylonian period, this phrase had many variants since it was not completely standardized.

4': we would expect gaba-ri kišib-ba-na, but this same formula with -ni appears also in CBS 19762 (P230142), an exemplar of OB Nippur ki-ulutin-bi-še$_3$;[63] see also §9 and MS 3176/5 below.

§4 (o.ii. 8–19) Barley loan

o.ii.	8.	**1.**	5(aš) ⸢še gur⸣
	9.	**2.**	ki lu$_2$-^{d}⸢nuska⸣(PA.⸢NAM$_2$⸣)-[t]a
	10.	**3.**	^{I}⸢ur-^{d}⸣pa-b[il]-⸢saĝ-ĝa$_2$⸣
	11.	**4.**	⸢šu ba⸣-an-ti
	12.	**5.**	ud ⸢buru$_{14}$⸣-ka
	13.	**6.**	⸢šum$_2$⸣-mu-dam
	14.	**7.**	[tu]kum-bi
	15.	**8.**	⸢ud-buru$_{14}$⸣-[ka]
	16.	**9.**	[la-ba-an]-⸢šum$_2$⸣
	17.	**10.**	[še maš$_2$ ĝa$_2$]-⸢ĝa$_2$$^{?}$-dam⸣
	18.	**11.**	[lu$_2$-ki-inim]-⸢ma⸣
	19.	**12.**	[iti-bi mu-bi]

"3–4Ur-Pabilsaĝa has received 2from Lu-Nuska 15 *gur* of barley; 5–6to be given (back) at harvest time. 7–10If he [does not] give it back [at] harvest time, [the barley (and its) interest] are to be paid. 11–12[(Its) witnesses its month, its year]".

Notes

2: for the use of the orthography PA.NAM$_2$/PA.UDU with the values /nuska/ and /enšadu/ in the Old Babylonian lexical lists from Nippur, see Peterson 2009: 68.

§5 (o.iii. 1–5) Barley loan

			the contract begins in the previous column
o.iii.	1.	**1'.**	šu ⸢ba⸣-an-ti
	2.	**2'.**	[iti] ⸢šeg$_{12}$-a⸣-ka

---

[60] Cf. Steinkeller 2002: 113–114.

[61] *OrSP* 47–49 411: 7-9; *TMH* NF 1–2 47: 10–13; *NRVN* 1 244: 6–8.

[62] Spada 2011 § 5; and some unpublished model contracts, such as MS 3179 (prism; P342646) Side B ii. 1'–7'; N 1323 (P230643) o.ii.' 4–17; X.3.217 (prism; P433189) Side C ii' 1'–6'.

[63] Cf. DCCLT (http://oracc.org/dcclt/P230142).

3. **3'.** ⸢šum$_2$-mu⸣-dam
4. **4'.** lu$_2$-ki-⸢inim⸣-ma
5. **5'.** ⸢iti-bi⸣ mu-bi

"[PN$_2$] $^{1'}$has received [x *gur* of barley, from PN$_1$]; $^{2'–3'}$to be given (back) in the third [month]. $^{4'–5'}$(Its) witnesses, its month, its year".

§6 (o.iii. 6–17) Barley loan

o.iii. 6. **1.** 1(aš)+⸢x⸣ še gur
7. **2.** [maš$_2$ 1(aš) gu]r 1(barig) 4(ban$_2$) še-ta-am$_3$
8. **3.** [sig$_9$-g]e$_4$-de$_3$
9. **4.** k[i] ^{d}nanna-⸢me⸣-ša$_4$-ta
10. **5.** ^{I}*i*[*n-b*]*i*-⸢*i*$_3$⸣-*li*$_2$-*šu* dumu *gur*-⸢*ru*$^?$⸣-*um*
11. **6.** šu [ba]-an-ti
12. **7.** [mu še] ⸢u$_3$⸣ [maš$_2$] nu-mu-un-sug$_6$-a-⸢še$_3$$^?$⸣
13. **8.** ⸢5⸣ giĝ$_4$ ⸢kug⸣-babbar
14. **9.** *ši-pi*$_2$-*ir-tum*-še$_3$
15. **10.** ⸢in-na⸣-an-⸢tak$_4$⸣
16. **11.** ⸢x x x⸣
17. **12.** [...] ⸢x⸣ [x]

rest of column broken

"$^{5–6}$I[nb]i-ilīšu, son of Gurrum, has received ^{4}from Nanna-meša $^{1–3}$[x]+1 *gur* of barley, – [an interest rate] of 1 *barig* 4 *ban* (= 100 *sila*) of barley per [1 *gu*]*r* is to be [charged]; ^{7}[since] he did not repay [the barley] and [(its) interest], ^{10}he has left to him $^{8–9}$5 shekels of silver as a pledge ...".

Notes

7–10: a very similar situation seems to be recorded in another model contract appearing in the micro-tablet MS 3176/5[64] (the transliteration of which is offered below). There it is said that, since a debtor did not repay his debt (a ridiculously low amount of barley: 1 *sila*, equivalent to 1 litre) to the creditor, he has left him an unweighed block of silver (Sumerian kug pad-ra$_2$, equated to the Akkadian *šibirtu*) as security, until the debt is repaid in full.[65]

9: the term *šipirtu* seems to be a variant of the Akkadian term *šiprūtu*, which, according to Westbrook (2001: 65), "was apparently the standard term for pledge of movable objects, mentioned occasionally in letters".[66] For this term cf. also Charpin 1990: 256–257, Charpin 2009 and Charpin 2015: 176.

MS 3176/5 (o.iii'. 1–12)

o.iii'. 1. **1.** 1(diš) sila$_3$ še
2. **2.** ĝiškim-ti-še$_3$
3. **3.** ki ^{d}mar-tu-zi-ĝu$_{10}$
4. **4.** ^{Id}mar-tu-*ba-ni*-ke$_4$

[64] See fn. 58 above.

[65] A similar phraseology also occurs in FLP 1287 vi 42–48 (cf. Roth 1979: 45 and 87) and Ai III ii 11–13.

[66] For the variant *šipirtu* of the term for "pledge", *šapartu*, in Old, Middle and Assyrian terminology cf. Radner 2001: 269 fn. 25.

5. **5.** šu ba-an-ti
6. **6.** mu še nu-mu-un-sug$_6$-ga-/še$_3^?$
7. **7.** kug pad-ra$_2$
8. **8.** ki-la$_2$ nu-mu-un-tag-ga
9. **9.** in-na-an-tak$_4$
10. **10.** ud še ba-ab-šum$_2$-mu-še$_3$
11. **11.** kug pad-ra$_2$-bi
12. **12.** ba-an-tum$_2$-mu

"$^{4-5}$Amurrum-bāni has received ^{3}from Martu-ziĝu $^{1-2}$1 *sila* of barley on trust; ^{6}since he (= Martu-ziĝu) did not repay the barley, ^{9}he has left (as security) $^{7-8}$an unprocessed and unweighed lump of silver; $^{10-12}$when the barley is given back, he (= the creditor) will bring (to the debtor) this unprocessed lump of silver".

§7 (o.iv. 1–9) Partnership loan

the contract begins in the previous column

o.iv. 1. **1'.** eš$_2$-⸢gar$_3$⸣-ne-⸢ne⸣
2. **2'.** un-til-le-eš
3. **3'.** ⸢šag$_4$⸣ dam-gar$_3$-ra-ke$_4$-ne
4. **4'.** ba-ab-dug$_3$-ge-eš
5. **5'.** a$_2$-tuku ĝal$_2$-la-bi
6. **6'.** min$_3$-na-ne-ne teš$_2$-a si$_3$-ga-bi
7. **7'.** i$_3$-ba-e-ne
8. **8'.** ⸢lu$_2$⸣-ki-inim-ma
9. **9'.** iti-bi mu-bi

"... $^{1'-2'}$since (or once) having finished their work assignment, $^{3'-4'}$they have satisfied the merchants. $^{5'-7'}$As many profits as there may be, the two of them will divide equally among themselves. $^{8'-9'}$(Its) witnesses, its month, its year".

Notes

Notwithstanding only its final section being preserved, this model contract can likely be identified as a partnership loan (see the commentary to **2** §2 above).

3': surely šag$_4$ dam-gar$_3$-ra-ke$_4$-ne is a scribal mistake, since we expect here a form like šag$_4$ dam-gar$_3$-ra-ne (< dam-gar$_3$+ene+ak), "(they have satisfied) the heart of the merchants". In any case, in this kind of texts usually this formula refers to a single merchant.

5'–7': this standard profit-clause, which appears also in the partnership loan contracts §10 and §11 (see below), is rather frequent in model contracts from Nippur recording commercial loans;[67] moreover, it can be found also in two functional contracts from Nippur.[68]

The term a$_2$-tuku (Akk. *nēmelu*), at line 5', means "surplus, profit from partnership and other business ventures" (cf. CAD N$_2$, p. 157ff).

[67] CBS 9852+ (P230749) r.i. 31'–34'; CBS 10252 (P230621) ii. 10'–13'; MS 3333 (P252274) r. 4–9; UM 29-15-997 (P230635) r.i'. 7'–10'.

[68] PBS 8/2 151 (P262171) r. 1–3 and N 994 (P276142) r. 1'–3'.

§8 (o.iv. 10–16) Silver loan

o.iv.	10.	**1.**	1 giĝ$_4$ kug-babbar
	11.	**2.**	maš$_2$ 1 giĝ$_4$ igi 6-ĝal$_2$ ⸢6⸣ še kug-babbar
	12.	**3.**	taḫ-ḫe-dam
	13.	**4.**	ki ^{d}utu-ma-an-šum$_2$-⸢ta⸣
	14.	**5.**	⸢^{I}*a-gu*⸣-*u*$_2$-*a*-⸢ke$_4$⸣
	15.	**6.**	[šu b]a-an-t[i]
	16.	**7.**	[...] ⸢x x⸣
			rest of column missing

"$^{5-6}$Agū'a [has recei]ved ^{4}from Utu-manšum $^{1-3}$1 shekel of silver, – an interest rate of $^{1}/_{6}$ (of shekel) and 6 grains per 1 shekel is to be added ...".

Notes

2: 20% is the regular rate of interest for silver loans in the Old Babylonian period. This "particularly unusual mode of expressing the 20% interest rate on silver loans" (Skaist 1994: 106), i.e. 1 giĝ$_4$ igi-6-ĝal$_2$ 6 še, appears both in the Code of Hammurapi and in the Laws of Ešnunna.[69] However, according to Skaist, it "does not reflect the practice of the loan contracts at the times when the codes were promulgated. Nor does this formula occur in *ana ittišu*. There are available only six loan contracts[70] which use this particular interest rate formula". This formula appears also in two more model contracts (Wilson 2008 no. 54 and 179) and probably in YBC 263: 2 (= Bodine 2015: 47).[71]

§9 (o.v. 1–15) Silver loan

o.v.	1.	**1.**	6 giĝ$_4$ kug-babbar
	2.	**2.**	maš$_2$ 10 giĝ$_4$ 2 giĝ$_4$ kug-babbar-ta-am$_3$
	3.	**3.**	taḫ-ḫe-dam
	4.	**4.**	ki e$_2$-lu$_2$-ti-⸢ta⸣
	5.	**5.**	^{Id}nanna-me-ša$_4$-ke$_4$
	6.	**6.**	šu ba-an-ti
	7.	**7.**	kug u$_3$ maš$_2$-bi
	8.	**8.**	šag$_4$ e$_2$-lu$_2$-ti-ke$_4$
	9.	**9.**	al-⸢dug$_3$⸣
	10.	**10.**	kišib-bi ki e$_2$-lu$_2$-t[i-ta]
	11.	**11.**	u$_2$-gu ba-an-⸢de$_2$⸣
	12.	**12.**	gaba-ri kišib-ba-ni
	13.	**13.**	i[n-na]-an-tak$_4$
	14.	**14.**	[ud kur$_2$]-še$_3$
	15.	**15.**	[kišib ul-pad$_3$ zi-re]-⸢dam⸣

[69] Laws of Ešnunna §18A: 1 GIĜ$_4$ IGI.6.ĜAL$_2$ *u*$_3$ 6 ŠE MAŠ$_2$ *u*$_2$-*ṣa-ab*; Code of Hammurapi §L: *šum-ma* KUG.BABBAR *a-na* UR$_5$.RA *id-di-in a-na* 1 GIĜ$_4$ KUG.BABBAR^{im} IGI.6.ĜAL$_2$ *u*$_3$ 6 ŠE MAŠ$_2$^{am} *i-le-eq-qe*$_2$.

[70] To the six loan contracts cited by Skaist, eight more contracts from Kisurra, published by Goddeeris 2009, are to be added: SANTAG 9, 105, 136, 137, 140, 199, 205, 214, 253.

[71] See Spada 2017b: 299–300 for this hypothesis.

"[5–6]Nanna-meša has received [4]from Eluti [1–3]6 shekels of silver, – an interest rate of 2 shekels of silver per 10 shekels is to be added; [7–9]the silver and its interest have satisfied Eluti. [10–11]Its (= of the repayment) sealed tablet has been lost from (the house of) Eluti (so that) [12–13]he (= Eluti) has drawn up [for him (= Nanna-meša)] a copy of his sealed tablet. [14–15]In [the future], should the [lost tablet be found, it has to be destroyed]".

Notes

Duplicates of this model contract appear in two multi-column tablets: UM 29-13-408a (from Nippur), and MS 3176/5, both of them present few variants in the name of the debtor and the commodity lent (barley instead of silver).

2: this formula is recorded in Ai II i 42[72] and, according to A. Skaist, was found also in a few Ur III period loan contracts (Skaist 1994: 108).

Duplicates:

UM 29-13-408a (o.ii'. 4'–12')

o.ii'.	4'.	**1.**	1(u) 5(aš) [še gur]
	5'.	**2.**	ki e$_2$-lu$_2$-t[i-ta]
	6'.	**3.**	^{I}e$_2$-ur$_2$-bi-dug$_3$-k[e$_4$]
	7'.	**4.**	šu ba-an-ti
	8'.	**5.**	še u$_3$ maš$_2$-bi
	9'.	**6.**	šag$_4$ e$_2$-lu$_2$-ti-ke$_4$
	10'.	**7.**	al-dug$_3$
	11'.	**8.**	kišib-bi ki e$_2$-lu$_2$-ti-ta
	12'.	**9.**	u$_2$-gu ba-an-d[e$_2$]
			rest of column missing

[3–4]E-urbidug has received [2]from Eluti [1]15 [*gur* of barley]; [5–7]the barley and its interest have satisfied Eluti. [8–9]Its (= of the repayment) sealed tablet has been lost from (the house of) Eluti ..."

MS 3176/5 (o.iii'. 32–o.iv'. 2)

o.iii'.	32.	**1.**	[1(u) 5(aš)$^{?}$] še gur
	33.	**2.**	[maš$_2$ 1(aš) gur 1(barig)] 4(ban$_2$) še-ta
	34.	**3.**	[ki e$_2$-lu$_2$]-ti-ta
	35.	**4.**	[^{I}e$_2$-ur$_2$-bi]-dug$_3$-ke$_4$
	36.	**5.**	[šu ba-an]-ti
	37.	**6.**	[še u$_3$ maš$_2$]-bi
	38.	**7.**	[šag$_4$ e$_2$-lu$_2$]-ti
	39.	**8.**	[al-d]ug$_3$
	40.	**9.**	[kišib-bi ki e$_2$-lu$_2$-t]i
	41.	**10.**	[u$_2$-gu ba-an-de$_2$]
	42.	**11.**	[gaba-ri kišib-ba-n]i
	43.	**12.**	[in-na-an-tak$_4$]
o.iv'.	1.	**13.**	ud kur$_2$-še$_3$
	2.	**14.**	kišib ul-pa zi-re-dam

[72] The other two percentage formulas recorded in Ai. are: maš$_2$ 1 giĝ$_4$ igi-5-ĝal$_2$ še-ta-am$_3$ and maš$_2$ 1 ma-na 12 giĝ$_4$-ta-am$_3$ (in Ai II i 41 and 43 respectively).

“[$^{4-5}$E-urbi]dug ha[s received] ^{3}from [Elu]ti $^{1-2}$[15$^{?}$] *gur* of barley – [an interest rate of 1 *barig*] 4 *ban* (= 100 *sila*) [per 1 *gur* of] barley (is to be added); $^{6-8}$[the barley and] its [interest have satisfied Elu]ti. $^{9-12}$[Its (= of the repayment) sealed tablet has been lost from (the house of) Elut]i, [(so that) he (= Eluti) has drawn up for him (= E-urbidug) a copy of his sealed tablet]. $^{13-14}$In the future, should the (lost) tablet be found, it has to be destroyed”.

§10 (r.i. 1’–10’) Partnership loan

r.i. 1’. **1.** ⸢1⸣ [ma-na kug-babbar]
2’. **2.** še [sa$_{10}$-sa$_{10}$-de$_{3}$]
3’. **3.** ki ⸢^{d}EN.ZU⸣-[...-ta]
4’. **4.** ^{Id}EN.⸢ZU-*re*$^{?}$⸣-[*me*$^{?}$-*ni*$^{?}$]
5’. **5.** šu ba-[an-ti]
6’. **6.** iti šeg$_{12}$-a-[ka]
7’. **7.** kug-bi šum$_{2}$-m[u-dam]
8’. **8.** a$_{2}$-tuku ĝal$_{2}$-l[a-bi]
9’. **9.** min$_{3}$-na-ne-ne teš$_{2}$-a si$_{3}$-g[a-bi]
10’. **10.** i$_{3}$-ba-e-ne

“$^{4-5}$Sîn-rē[mēni$^{?}$ has re]ceived ^{3}from Sîn-[...] $^{1-2}$1 [mina of silver for buying] barley; $^{6-7}$the silver is to be paid (back) in the third month. $^{8-10}$As many profits as there may be, the two of them will divide equally among themselves”.

Notes

This model contract can be considered a partnership loan, even if the formula nam-tab-ba-še$_{3}$ (“for a partnership enterprise”) does not appear.
2: the expression (here completed on the basis of §12: 3) specifies the purpose for which the loan is made. It appears also in another unpublished model contract from Nippur (N 3472 o. 2, P230659). In §11: 3, instead, the expression kiĝ$_{2}$ ak-de$_{3}$, “for doing a work” appears.
In other model contracts the following similar expressions occur:

- kaš sa$_{10}$-sa$_{10}$-de$_{3}$, “for buying beer”: CBS 2298 o. 3, 10, 13; MS 2348 (P251568) o.i 7’; MS 3176/5 o.ii’ 3 and r.iii 36; UM 29-15-830 (P230632) o. 2;
- ^{še}ĝeš-i$_{3}$ sa$_{10}$-sa$_{10}$-de$_{3}$, “for buying sesame”: CBS 3867 (P230728) o.ii’. 5’;
- tug$_{2}$ sa$_{10}$-sa$_{10}$-de$_{3}$, “for buying garments”: MS 3176/5 r.ii. 21.

Sometimes, the purpose of trade is implicit in the clause of term of repayment, where the expression kaskal silim-ma, “on safe completion of the (commercial) expedition” appears; cf. MS 3333 (P252274) o. 20, and TLB 1 266 (P390404) o. 7.

§11 (r.i. 11’–23’) Partnership loan

r.i. 11’. **1.** 2 ma-na kug-babbar
12’. **2.** nam-tab-ba-še$_{3}$
13’. **3.** kiĝ$_{2}$ ak-de$_{3}$
14’. **4.** ki ^{d}en-lil$_{2}$-ḫe$_{2}$-ĝal$_{2}$-ta
15’. **5.** ^{I}a-ba-^{d}en-lil$_{2}$-gin$_{7}$-ke$_{4}$
16’. **6.** šu ba-an-ti
17’. **7.** kug-bi sam$_{2}^{am3}$ kur$_{2}$-še$_{3}$
18’. **8.** nu-ĝa$_{2}$-ĝa$_{2}$-a
19’. **9.** kiĝ$_{2}$-bi lu$_{2}$-kur$_{2}$-še$_{3}$
20’. **10.** nu-mu-ni-in-šum$_{2}$

21'. **11.** a$_2$-tuku ĝal$_2$-⸢la⸣-bi
22'. **12.** teš$_2$-a si$_3$-⸢ga⸣-bi
23'. **13.** i$_3$-ba-⸢e⸣-ne

"$^{5–6}$Aba-Enlil-gin has received ^{4}from Enlil-ḫeĝal $^{1–3}$2 minas of silver for a partnership enterprise, for doing some work. $^{7–8}$He must not use (lit. put) that silver in order to buy other (goods), $^{9–10}$nor will he subcontract (lit. give) this work to another man. $^{11–13}$As many profits as there may be, they will divide equally among themselves".

Notes
3: this expression, specifying the purpose for which the loan is made, appears also in another model contact (Wilson 2008 no. 53 o. 15), the provenience of which is unknown.

§12 (r.i. 24'–28') Partnership loan

r.i. 24'. **1.** 3 ma-na ⸢kug⸣-babbar
25'. **2.** nam-tab-ba-še$_3$
26'. **3.** še sa$_{10}$-sa$_{10}$-de$_3$
27'. **4.** ki lu$_2$-^{d}EN.ZU-ta
28'. **5.** ^{I}⸢KA-^{d}nin-urta⸣ / u$_3$ ur-kingala(GAL.UKKIN)
rest missing

"^{5}KA-Ninurta and Ur-kingala [have received] ^{4}from Awīl-Sîn $^{1-3}$3 minas of silver for a partnership enterprise of buying barley ...".

§13 (r.ii. 1'–18') Rental of a house for storing barley

r.ii. [...]
1'. **1'.** še ⸢e$_2$$^{?}$⸣-l[u$_2$-bi]-⸢nu⸣-šub-bu
2'. **2'.** ^{I}lu$_2$-^{d}dumu-zi-da
3'. **3'.** ba-an-gu$_7$
4'. **4'.** mu še-bi in-gu$_7$-a-aš
5'. **5'.** di-kud-e-ne
6'. **6'.** 2(u) še gur
7'. **7'.** ^{I}lu$_2$-^{d}dumu-zi-da-ra
8'. **8'.** al-aĝ$_2$-de$_3$
9'. **9'.** inim$^{!}$ in-na-an-ne-eš
10'. **10'.** še-ga-ne-ne-ta
11'. **11'.** 1$^{?}$(u) 4$^{?}$(aš) še gur
12'. **12'.** ⸢iti⸣ šu-numun-a-ka
13'. **13'.** ^{I}lu$_2$-^{d}dumu-zi-da
14'. **14'.** lugal e$_2$-a-ke$_2$
15'. **15'.** ^{I}e$_2$$^{?}$-lu$_2$-bi-nu-šub-bu
16'. **16'.** lugal še-še$_3$ al-aĝ$_2$-e
17'. **17'.** inim-inim-ni ba-an-šum$_2$
18'. **18'.** mu lugal-bi in-pad$_3$

"...$^{2'–3'}$Lu-Dumuzida took for himself $^{1'}$the barley of El[ubi]-nušubbu$^{?}$; $^{4'}$since he took that barley, $^{5'}$the judges $^{9'}$have ordered $^{7'–8'}$Lu-Dumuzida to pay $^{6'}$20 *gur* of barley; $^{10'}$as mutually agreed, $^{12'}$in the fourth month, $^{13'–14'}$Lu-Dumuzida, the owner of the house $^{16'}$will pay $^{11'}$14$^{?}$ *gur* of barley $^{15'–16'}$to Elubi-nušubbu$^{?}$, the owner of the barley; $^{17'}$he has promised (lit: he has gave to him his spoken word); $^{18'}$he has sworn by the name of the king".

Notes

Unfortunately, the first part of this text is broken and it is not easy to fully understand what is recorded in it; therefore the above translation is to be considered as tentative.

Apparently, Elubi-nušubbu$^{?}$, "the owner of the barley" (lugal še, l. 16'), has stored his barley in the house of Lu-Dumuzida, "the owner of the house" (lugal e$_2$-a, l. 14'). It seems that Lu-Dumuzida has taken for himself (lit. "has eaten") the barley deposited in his house and the judges have therefore ordered to him to repay 20 *gur* of barley to the legitimate owner. This decision notwithstanding, the two protagonists agreed that Lu-Dumuzida would return only 14 *gur*.

3'–4': for the meaning "to take for oneself, to enjoy (something or the use of something), to use" of the verb gu$_7$, see CAD A$_1$ *s.v. akālu*, 2, p. 251f.

16': the use of the terminative posposition -še$_3$ with a profession term, instead of the dative posposition -ra is not unusual in the Old Babylonian model contracts.[73]

§14 (r.ii. 19'–29') Dissolution of a partnership

r.ii.	19'.	**1.**	1 $^{1}/_{2}$ ma-na kug-babbar
	20'.	**2.**	sig$_9$-ga *ma-nu-um-ba-lu*-AN
	21'.	**3.**	2 $^{1}/_{2}$ ma-na kug-babbar
	22'.	**4.**	sig$_9$-ga ur-^{d}⸢saman$^{?}$⸣(<EŠ>.⸢SUD⸣.NUN.⸢EŠ$_2$⸣<.TU>)-na
	23'.	**5.**	nam-tab-ba-še$_3$
	24'.	**6.**	šu-še$_3$$^{!}$(ŠU) in-ĝar-re-eš
	25'.	**7.**	ud sig$_9$-ga-ne-ne-a
	26'.	**8.**	niĝ$_2$-ŠID igi ^{d}utu-še$_3$
	27'.	**9.**	mu-un-ĝar-re-eš
	28'.	**10.**	⸢niĝ$_2$⸣ gub-ba ĝal$_2$-la-bi
	29'.	**11.**	kug-bi gi-na šu ba-ab-šum$_2$

"$^{1–2}$1 and $^{1}/_{2}$ minas of silver, the investment share of Mannum-balu-ilim, $^{3–4}$2 and $^{1}/_{2}$ minas of silver, the investment share of Ur-Samana, ^{6}they had put in (each other's) hands (i.e. had made it available to each other) ^{5}for a partnership enterprise. $^{7–9}$On the day when they have put before Šamaš the (final) balance of their investment shares, $^{10–11}$the silver which remains (= the profit), as much as it was available, has been handed over (to each) proportionally$^{?}$.

Notes

This text records the dissolution of a commercial partnership. As Dole notes, the *nikkassu* texts record the termination of partnerships (e.g. BE 6/1 15) focusing upon the final division of goods. The actual accounting took place in a temple, with the god as witness to the complete declaration of the profit (Dole 1965, 42ff.).

2 and **4**: for this term cf. the commentary to **2** §5: 2; this same terminology occurs also in UET 5 432.

[73] Cf., e.g., CUNES 52-08-065 Side B i. 8'; CUNES 52-10-147+ Side A ii. 7' (for the edition of these model contracts see fn. 59 above).

4: this same personal name appears in Goddeeris 2016 n. 5: 32.
8–9: see also Ai VI i 22–23: igi ^{d}utu-ke$_4$ / niĝ$_2$-ŠID-bi ab-ak-e-⸢ne⸣ / ⸢*i-na ma*⸣*-ḫa-ar* ^{d}UTU / ⸢NIĜ$_2$⸣-ŠID-*šu-nu ip-pu-šu*.
10: to the best of my knowledge, the term niĝ$_2$ gub-ba is rarely attested and its exact meaning is not completely understood (cf. Durand 1990: 300 fn. 70). Based on the context, it is understood here with the meaning of "the goods/possessions present", i.e. "what remains, the profit".
11: the Sumerian term gi-na seems here to have an adverbial value, comparable to the Akkadian *kīniš*, "duly, according to expectation, correctly" (cf. CAD K p. 385), in this case "proportionally".

§15 (r.ii. 30'–r.iii. 17') Rental of a house

r.ii.	30'.	**1.**	4(diš) sar e$_2$ du$_3$-a
	31'.	**2.**	⸢zag⸣-bi šeg$_{12}$ al-ur$_3$-ra
			unknown number of lines missing
r.iii.	1'.	**3'.**	ki [KA].⸢KA⸣-[ni-ma-an-šum$_2$-t]a
	2'.	**4'.**	^{I}*im-gur-*^{d}EN.ZU-ke$_4$
	3'.	**5'.**	ib$_2$-ta-an-e$_3$
	4'.	**6'.**	ezen diĝir-ra iti 4-kam
	5'.	**7'.**	1 ^{dug}kab$_2$-dug$_4$-ga
	6'.	**8'.**	1 laḫtan$_6$ MA$^?$
	7'.	**9'.**	1 laḫtan$_6$ TI LAM
	8'.	**10'.**	niĝ$_2$-gur$_{11}$ teš$_2$$^?$
	9'.	**11'.**	TUR MUNUS PI NA
	10'.	**12'.**	šu ba-ra-ab-tak$_4$
	11'.	**13'.**	^{I}*im-gur-*^{d}EN-ZU-e
	12'.	**14'.**	^{I}KA.KA-ni-ma-an-šum$_2$
	13'.	**15'.**	ur$_2$ e$_2$-a
	14'.	**16'.**	bi$_2$-ib-ku-šu-re
	15'.	**17'.**	ur$_3$ e$_2$-a im-ĝa$_2$-ĝa$_2$
	16'.	**18'.**	lu$_2$-⸢ki-inim⸣-ma
	17'.	**19'.**	iti-bi mu-bi

"$^{4'–5'}$Imgur-Sîn has rented $^{3'}$from [Kakani-manšum] $^{1'–2'}$a built-up house plot of 4 *sar* (= 144 m^2), the sides of which (are made of) kiln-fired bricks [...]; $^{6'}$during$^?$ the divine festival of the fourth month $^{12'}$he$^?$ will deliver $^{7'}$1 gauged measuring vessel, $^{8'}$1 ...-vat, $^{9'}$1 ...-vat: $^{10'–11'}$all these assets$^?$... $^{13'}$Imgur-Sîn $^{16'}$will repair $^{15'}$the foundations of the house (and) $^{17'}$will build (*lit.* place, set) the roof of the house $^{14'}$for Kakani-manšum. $^{18'–19'}$(Its) witnesses, its month, its year".

Notes
2: šeg$_{12}$ al-ur$_3$-ra, Akk. *agurru*, Type 8 according to the terminology assigned to each type of bricks by Powell (1982: 119), has a square upper surface measuring 20×20×5 fingers (33×33×8 cm) and seems to have been an ordinary house brick that was not given any special treatment such as backing or stamping.[74]
7': for this vessel cf. Sallaberger 1996: 45–46 and Civil 1994: 162–163.

74 Cf. Stol 2017: 273.

10': to the best of my knowledge, this terminology for property appears only once in school context: IM 70209 (o.iii. 14), a large multi-column tablet collecting legal phraseology, from Tell-Dhiba'i in the Baghdad area (cf. Al-Fouadi 1976: 2). According to N. Veldhuis it represents an entirely independent tradition from the two more standardized versions (the northern one, primarily known from Sippar, and the Nippur version) of Old Babylonian Legal Phrasebooks (cf. Veldhuis 2014: 188–194).
11': unfortunately, I cannot find any satisfactory solution to this line.
13'–17': in these lines there is a clause describing the works which have to be done by the tenant, Imgur-Sîn.[75]
The verbal form in line 16', bi$_2$-ib-ku-šu-re contains the Sumerian verb *kušur (written syllabically ku-šu.r), which, to the best of my knowledge, is attested in only three more examples, all of them appearing in Old Babylonian Nippur documents.[76] For the hypothesis that this Sumerian verb can be interpreted as an Akkadian loanword and related to the root **kšr*, attested in the verb *kašāru/kuššuru* (cf. CAD K, *s.v.* *kašāru* A, p. 284f.), meaning "to repair (ruined or damaged walls, building, ...)", see Spada 2017a.

§16 (r.iii. 18'–28') Sale of a field

r.iii.	18'.	**1.**	1(bur$_3$) GAN$_2$ a-šag$_4$ NUMUN$_2$.ŠE
	19'.	**2.**	šag$_4$ a-šag$_4$ šu-i
	20'.	**3.**	us$_2$-a-du ^{d}EN.ZU-*še-mi*
	21'.	**4.**	a-šag$_4$ lu$_2$-ur-saĝ-gal-zu
	22'.	**5.**	ki ⸢lu$_2$⸣-ur-saĝ-gal-zu-ta
	23'.	**6.**	^{I}*zi-ib-ba-*⸢*at*$^{?}$⸣-^{d}lamma$^{?}$
	24'.	**7.**	in-ši-in-sa$_{10}$
	25'.	**8.**	sam$_2$-til-la-bi-še$_3$
	26'.	**9.**	1 ma-na kug-babbar
	27'.	**10.**	in-na-an-la$_2$
	28'.	**11.**	ud kur$_2$-še$_3$
			rest missing

"$^{6-7}$Zibbat$^{?}$-Lamassi$^{?}$ has bought ^{5}from Lu-ursaĝgalzu $^{1-4}$a field in stubble of 1 *bur*$_3$ (= 6.48 ha.) in the irrigation district of "the barber", (its) flank bordering (the field) of Sîn-šēmi, (which is) the field of Lu-ursaĝgalzu; $^{8-10}$he has paid to him 1 mina of silver as its full price; ^{11}in the future ...".

Notes
1: for a-šag$_4$ NUMUN$_2$.ŠE (Akk. *urbatānu*), "field in stubble," see Klein–Sharlach 2007: 22, comm. to lines 44 and 49.
6: to the best of my knowledge, a similar personal name is not attested elsewhere, therefore its reading is here tentative.

§17 (r.iv. 1'–11') Sale of an orchard

r.iv.			*unknown number of lines missing*
	1'.	**1'.**	[ki ^{d}EN.ZU-*i-din-nam*-t]a
	2'.	**2'.**	[^{I}*a-wi*]-⸢*il*⸣-*i*$_3$-*li*$_2$-ke$_4$

[75] See Stol 1993–1995: 165b–166a.
[76] CBS 7580 and UM 29-15-855 (= Robertson 1984: 169 and 170); HS 2021 (= Goddeeris 2016: 250f.).

3'.	**3'.**	[in-š]i-in-sa$_{10}$
4'.	**4'.**	[sa]m$_2$-til-la-bi-še$_3$
5'.	**5'.**	⸢$^1/_2$⸣ ma-na kug-babbar
6'.	**6'.**	in-na-an-la$_2$
7'.	**7'.**	ud kur$_2$-še$_3$
8'.	**8'.**	^{Id}EN.ZU-*i-din-nam*
9'.	**9'.**	^{ĝeš}kiri$_6$-še$_3$
10'.	**10'.**	inim nu-um-ĝa$_2$-ĝa$_2$-a
11'.	**11'.**	mu lugal-bi in-pad$_3$

"$^{2'-3'}$[Awī]l-ilī has bought $^{1'}$from [Sîn-iddinam an orchard ...] (and) $^{4'-6'}$he has paid to him half a mina of silver as its full price. $^{11'}$He (= Sîn-iddinam) has sworn by the name of the king that $^{7'-10'}$in the future Sîn-iddinam shall not raise a claim concerning (this) orchard".

§18 (r.iv. 12'–24') Silver loan with a pledge

r.iv.	12'.	**1.**	$^1/_2$ ma-na kug-babbar
	13'.	**2.**	ki lu$_2$-i$_3$-si-in^{ki}-na-ta
	14'.	**3.**	^{I}*a-ḫu-*⸢*šu*⸣*-nu*-ke$_4$
	15'.	**4.**	šu ba-an-ti
	16'.	**5.**	maš$_2$-bi-še$_3$
	17'.	**6.**	2(diš) sar e$_2$ du$_3$-a
	18'.	**7.**	da e$_2$ *a-bu-um-wa-qar*
	19'.	**8.**	e$_2$ *a-ḫu-šu-nu*
	20'.	**9.**	kug-ta ib$_2$-ta-gub
	21'.	**10.**	ud kug mu-un-tum$_3$-da
	22'.	**11.**	e$_2$-a-ni-še$_3$ ba-an-ku$_4$-ku$_4$
	23'.	**12.**	lu$_2$-ki-inim-⸢ma⸣
	24'.	**13.**	iti-bi mu-bi

"$^{3-4}$Aḫušunu has received ^{2}from Lu-Isinna ^{1}half a mina of silver; $^{5-9}$as its interest, a built-up house plot of 2 *sar*, next to the house of Abum-waqar, (which is) the house of Aḫušunu, will serve as a pledge. $^{10-11}$When he (= Aḫušunu) brings the silver, he can enter (again) into his house. $^{12-13}$(Its) witnesses, its month, its year".

Notes

9: this is the standard Sumerian formula for a pledge, in its shortened form (for an example of its fullest form see **5** §1: 12–13 below). Usually, but not invariably, a further formula (maš$_2$-bi-še$_3$, "for its interest") is added in order to show that the pledge is antichretic; this is the case in l. 5. The object of a pledge may be land or persons (wives, sons, daughters, male or female slaves, and even the debtor himself). For detailed studies of the Old Babylonian pledge documents see Kienast 1978: 66–103 and Skaist 1994: 202–230; see also Westbrook 2001: 63–79 and Veenhof 2004: 443–445.

§19 (r.iv. 25') Silver loan

r.iv.	25'.	**1.**	$^2/_3$ ma-na kug-babbar
			rest missing

"^{1}Two third of mina of silver...".

§20 (r.v. 1'–10') Repayment of a silver loan

r.v. *unknown number of lines missing*

1'. **1'.** [...] ⸢x⸣
2'. **2'.** [...] kug-babbar
3'. **3'.** [in-n]a$^{?}$-su-su-e
4'. **4'.** [m]u-a 4 kam-ma-še$_3$
5'. **5'.** ⸢kug⸣-bi al-til-la$^{!}$
6'. **6'.** ⸢ki ur⸣-^{d}nuska-ta
7'. **7'.** $^{[I]}$*i*$_3$-*li*$_2$-tab-ba-*e*-e
8'. **8'.** ⸢šu ba⸣-an-ti
9'. **9'.** ⸢lu$_2$⸣-ki-inim-ma
10'. **10'.** iti-bi mu-bi

"... $^{2'–3'}$[tot.] silver he should have returned [to hi]m. $^{4'}$By the fourth ye[ar] $^{6'–8'}$Ilī-tappê has received from Ur-Nuska $^{5'}$this silver, which has been paid in full. $^{9'–10'}$(Its) witnesses, its month, its year".

Notes

There is a possibility that the previous text, §19, is the beginning of this contract. However, being unable to establish it with certainty, I keep the two contracts separate.

5': for the Sumerian verb til, Akkadian *gummuru*, "to pay (back) in full", cf. CAD G, *s. v. gamāru*, p. 30.

Colophon (r.v. 11'–13')

r.v. 11'. **1.** šu ur-du$_6$-ku$_3$-ga
12'. **2.** ⸢dub⸣-sar tur
13'. **3.** ⸢dumu⸣ ^{d}nuska-a$_2$-maḫ

"^{1}Hand of Ur-dukuga, ^{2}the junior scribe, ^{3}son of Nuska-amaḫ"

Notes

Among the school texts, Type I tablets and Prisms may have a colophon, which generally contains "para-textual" information, such as the name of the scribe (sometimes defined as dub-sar tur, "junior scribe"), with his patronymic, the number of lines or sections and occasionally may include a date (but no examples from Nippur have been found so far; cf. Veldhuis 1997: 30 and fn. 86). Colophons usually appear at the botton of the reverse of a tablet, being separated from the main text by a blank space, a single or double line (as in this case).

To the best of my knowledge, in the Nippur documentation there are no attestations of a certain Ur-dukuga, whose father is named Nuska-amaḫ.

Doxology (r.v. 14')

r.v. 14'. **1.** ^{d}nisaba za$_3$-mi$_2$

"Nisaba be praised!".

Notes

The colophon can also contain a doxology, which, in lexical texts, is usually a formula of praise to Nisaba, goddess of grain, writing, and wisdom, who was worshipped in Uruk, Umma, and other southern Mesopotamian cities, viz., ^{d}nisaba za$_{3}$-mi$_{2}$, “Nisaba be praised!”.[77] In the tablet presented here, the doxology addressed to Nisaba is separated from the colophon and the main text by a box-design, filling the empty space in the last column of the reverse.

[77] Whereas documents from Nippur only have ^{d}nisaba za$_{3}$-mi$_{2}$, texts from other places have different formulas, such as “by the life of Nisaba and Ḫaia” (ti-la ^{d}nisaba ^{d}ḫa-ia$_{3}$); for this doxology in model contracts cf. Bodine 2015: 130–131. For a list of doxologies in mathematical texts see Friberg 2007: 399 and Proust 2012.

3. Type II tablets

The following five tablets are identified as Type II tablets (or "Teacher-Student" tablets) within the classification proposed by M. Civil.
A Type II tablet is a medium-size tablet, on which different exercises are typically written on the obverse and reverse. On the obverse (conventionally labeled as II/1) the left column contains an extract of between 6 and 15 lines (or one-to-four model contracts) written by an instructor, with blank space to the right where the pupil could copy it multiple times, until he knew it by heart. Whereas the first column is usually preserved, the student's column was erased so that it could be used several times. As a result the right-hand side of the obverse is usually much thinner than the left-hand side. Moreover, very often the tablet was cut in two on purpose, probably to preserve the teacher's example on the left side. The reverse (II/2) is divided into three to five columns and may hold between 60 and 150 lines of text from a previously studied composition, usually written in a smaller, cursive script.
The obverse of tablets no. **5**, **6** and **7** contain several barley and silver loan contracts, whereas nos. **8** and **9**, unfortunately fragmentary, record respectively the lease of a real estate and a division of inheritance with supporting clause.
Apart from one tablet containing model contracts on both sides (no. **5**), the other tablets present on the reverse one of the advanced lists which were studied in the third phase of the curriculum:[78]

	Obverse	**Reverse**
5.	Silver loan with a pledge	Five silver loans
6.	Four barley loans	Nigga
7.	Silver loan with a pledge	OB Izi
8.	Lease of a real estate	OB Ura 5
9.	Division of inheritance	OB Nippur Ea

5.
Museum n°: HS 1770
Plates: 8–9 and 24–25
Measurements: 15.3×6.2×3.9 cm
State of preservation: left half of the entire tablet.

This tablet, which contains model contracts both on the obverse and the reverse, seems to have been cut in two on purpose, to preserve the teacher's example on the left side. As a consequence, part of the columns (in origin three or four) and the model contracts written on the reverse are missing.
The writing order on the obverse and reverse in this type of tablet is not always clear. In principle, the obverse is written before the reverse, but partially the process of writing and erasing of the right-hand column(s) on the obverse (which contributes to the fragility and vulnerability of the tablet to break in two) had to be done after the complete writing of the reverse.

[78] See the description of the Nippur scribal curriculum in Veldhuis 2014: 204–212.

Niek Veldhuis studied the Nippur Type II tablets and advanced the hypothesis that the reverse, written by the same student who had copied the model on the right column of the obverse, repeated extracts of a previously studied composition.
However, the tablet presented here seems not to follow this pattern. At least four out of six silver loans preserved on the tablet seem to be arranged on an ascending progression in the quantities of silver lent out: 12 shekels in the left-hand column of the obverse (the teacher's model), and, respectively, 15, 16 and 16 $^2/_3$ shekels in the following three contracts, written on the reverse, from right to left. On the basis of this progression, then, the exercises on the reverse would have been studied and written after (and not before) the model contract on the obverse.

§1 (o.i. 1–18) Silver loan with a pledge

o.i.	1.	**1.**	⸢12⸣ giĝ$_4$ kug-babbar
	2.	**2.**	šu-la$_2$ maš$_2$ nu-ub-tuku
	3.	**3.**	ki lu$_2$-^{d}nuska
	4.	**4.**	dumu lu$_2$-nin-mar-ki-ta
	5.	**5.**	^{I}puzur$_4$-^{d}nin-kar-ra-ak-ke$_4$
	6.	**6.**	šu ba-an-ti
	7.	**7.**	maš$_2$-bi-še$_3$ 1 saĝ-nita$_2$
	8.	**8.**	^{I}*i$_3$-li$_2$-⸢a⸣-a-ba-aš*
	9.	**9.**	⸢mu⸣-ni-im
	10.	**10.**	[arad$_2$] ⸢puzur$_4$⸣-^{d}nin-kar-ra-⸢ak⸣
	11.	**11.**	lu$_2$-^{d}nuska-ra
	12.	**12.**	kug-ta gub-ba-aš
	13.	**13.**	ib$_2$-ta-an-gub-bu
	14.	**14.**	⸢ud 1$^?$⸣-e a$_2$-ni-e
	15.	**15.**	kiĝ$_2$ a-šag$_4$-ga al-ak-e
	16.	**16.**	u$_3$ kiĝ$_2$-gi$_4$-a-še$_3$ al-DU
	17.	**17.**	ud kug mu-un-tum$_3$-da
	18.	**18.**	arad$_2$-da-ni ba-an-tum$_2$-mu

“[5–6]Puzur-Ninkarrak has received [3–4]from Lu-Nuska, son of Lu-Ninmarki [1–2]12 shekels of silver, as a *šula*-loan, without interest. [7–10]As its interest, a man named Ilī-aj-abāš, (who is) [the slave] of Puzur-Ninkarrak, [11–13]will serve as a pledge to Lu-Nuska. [14–16]As his daily chores, he (=Ilī-aj-abāš) will do the field-work and will perform the (house)-work. [17–18]When he (= Puzur-Ninkarrak) brings the silver, he can take back his slave”.

Notes

2: according to the CAD (CAD Q, *s.v. qīptu*, pp. 261f.), the Sumerian term šu-la$_2$ is “an amount of silver entrusted to an agent for buying goods to be sold on consignment or the consigned goods themselves, on which interest is not charged until a particular period (usually unspecified) has elapsed”, and it is often followed by the formula “without interest” (and this is the case here). Skaist (1994: 41–51), by examining the nature of the šu-la$_2$/*qīptu*-loan, highlighted some links between this type of loan and commerce: some loan contracts, in fact, seem to refer to a business journey made by the borrower; moreover, the term šu-la$_2$ appears also in some partnership loans.[79]

[79] For the partnership loans see the commentary to **2** §2, **4** §7, §10 and §14.

The substantial *qīptu*-loans are then meant for small investments or futher distribution,[80] and, therefore, the recipient or the creditor of the *qīptu*-loan was a middle-man. Some of the Kisurra loan contracts edited by Goddeeris in SANTAG 9 (nos. 151, 154, 178, 212, 217), seem to confirm Skaist's analysis, since they illustrate this re-distribution of the silver/barley amounts (cf. Goddeeris 2009: 177).

12–13: for the antichretic pledge see the commentary to **4** §18: 9 above.

14: instead of the expected terminative "-še$_3$",[81] here the locative-terminative "-e" is used to form the expression ud 1-e a$_2$-ni-e "as his daily chores".

16: to the best of my knowledge, a similar expression appears in only one other model contract (Wilson 2008 no. 180 o.i. 1'–20') recording the antichretic pledge of a slave-girl, who has to perform several tasks, the list of which ends with the formula kiĝ$_2$-gi$_4$-<a>-še$_3$ al-du$_3$-e (o.i. 15'–16'), likely translated as: "she will perform (these works) as (her) task".

The term kiĝ$_2$-gi$_4$-a is often equated to the Akkadian *šipru*, "work to be performed, task" (cf. CAD Š$_3$ p. 76ff.) and it has been translated here as "house-work", in order to distinguish it from the field-work mentioned in l. 15.

A similar formula occurs also in Ai VI iii 16–17: u$_3$ kiĝ$_2$-gi$_4$-a ba-ab-tum$_3$-mu, equated to the Akkadian *u$_3$ ši-ip-ra ub-bal*, translated by Landsberger as "und den Arbeitsauftrag wird er bekommen" (MSL 1, p. 83).

In contrast to the Ai passage, in both model contracts kiĝ$_2$-gi$_4$-a ends with the terminative "-še$_3$", the value of which is not completely understood here. Moreover, it is also unclear how to interpret the verb al-DU, whether as a phonetic variant of the Sumerian du$_3$, Akkadian *epēšu* (cf. CAD Š$_3$, *s.v. šipru* 3d), as in Wilson 2008 no. 180, or as al-tum$_2$, corresponding to the Akkadian verb *abālu*, as in the first millennium lexical series.

17–18: the reading and interpretation of the various forms of the verb "to bring" has been recently discussed by Sallaberger 2005 and Meyer-Laurin 2010 (cf. also Zólyomi 2017: 141–142). Sallaberger makes a distinction between the verbs de$_6$ and tum$_2$: the first one is used with persons, herd animals and boats (which can move on their own), whereas the second is used with objects (which must be carried). Meyer-Laurin focuses on two different meanings: "to lead" (tum$_2$) and "to deliver" (de$_6$/tum$_3$). In the present case, both theories seem to be confirmed.

o.i. 19. **1.** 12 giĝ$_4$ kug-babbar

Notes

This is a catchline, i.e. the last line on the tablet, but the first line of the next contract (not copied); it could appear in Type II and Type III tablets.

§2 (r.i'. 1–4) Silver loan

the contract begins in the previous column

r.i'. 1. **1'.** šu ba-a[n-ti]
2. **2'.** mu-DU [ud buru$_{14}$-ka]
3. **3'.** kug u$_3$ [maš$_2$-bi]
4. **4'.** i$_3$-la$_2$-[e]

[80] Cf. the Hammurapi Code, §107 (Roth 1995: 101) in which loans described with the verb *qâpu*, "to entrust", have a commercial nature.

[81] Cf. e.g. the expressions in PBS 13 39 (P230625, a collection of model contracts) o.i'. 9 and o.ii'. 4'. In N 4976 (P229570) o.i. 5, instead, ud 1-e a$_2$-ni-še$_3$ occurs.

"[PN$_2$ $^{1'}$has re]ceived [from PN$_1$ x shekels of silver]; $^{2'}$at the delivery [of the harvest] $^{4'}$he will pay back $^{3'}$the silver with [its interest]".

§3 (r.i'. 5–12) Silver loan

r.i'.	5.	**1.**	15$^{!}$ [giĝ$_4$ kug-babbar]
	6.	**2.**	en-n[u$^{?}$-...]
	7.	**3.**	$^{I?}$x$^{?}$ [...]
	8.	**4.**	da$^{?}$-⸢x$^{?}$⸣ [...]
	9.	**5.**	^{I}*i*$^{?}$-*d*[*in*$^{?}$-...]
	10.	**6.**	in-n[a-...]
	11.	**7.**	ud al-l[a$^{?}$-be$_2$-a]
	12.	**8.**	kug-bi ⸢i$_3$⸣-[na-ab-šum$_2$-mu]

"$^{1–4}$15$^{!}$ [shekels of silver], ...; $^{5–6}$Id[din$^{?}$-...], did ...; $^{7–8}$when he (= the creditor) re[quests it], he [will give to him] that silver".

Notes

7–8: due to the fragmentary nature of this text, not all the lines are understood; these two lines are tentatively restored based on similar clauses occurring in Ai,[82] which admittedly is much later. For a description of request formula in Old Babylonian loan contracts cf. Skaist 1994: 180–183.

§4 (r.i'. 13–24) Silver loan

r.i'.	13.	**1.**	⸢16$^{?}$⸣ giĝ$_4$ [kug-babbar]
	14.	**2.**	^{Id}en$^{?}$-[...-ke$_4$$^{?}$]
	15.	**3.**	^{I}ur-^{d}[...-ra]
	16.	**4.**	eš ib$_2$-[ta-de$_2$]
	17.	**5.**	iti udru^{duru5}-ka ⸢zal$^{?}$⸣-[la-ta$^{?}$]
	18.	**6.**	kug-bi i$_3$-[la$_2$-e]
	19.	**7.**	tuk[um(ŠU.ĜAR.T[UR.LAL])-bi]
	20.	**8.**	[it]i šeg$_{12}$-[a-ka]
	21.	**9.**	⸢iti$^{?}$⸣ [k]ug-babbar i[n-...]
	22.	**10.**	kug-bi la-[ba-an-la$_2$]
	23.	**11.**	maš$_2$ 10 giĝ$_4$ [2 giĝ$_4$-ta-am$_3$]
	24.	**12.**	bi$_2$-ib$_2$-[taḫ-e]

"$^{1–4}$PN gave 16 shekels [of silver ^{3}to] Ur-[...] as a loan; $^{5–6}$he (= Ur-[...]) [will pay] that silver by the end of the eleventh month. $^{7–10}$If in the third$^{!}$ mon[th, the month in which] the silver is [...], he will not [pay back] that silver, $^{11–2}$he [will add] an interest rate [of 2 shekels] per 10 shekels (of silver)".

[82] Ai III i 63–64: ud um-mi-a kug-bi al-la-be$_2$-a / kug-bi an-na-ab-šum$_2$-m[u] / *i-n*[*u um-mi-a-nu* KUG.BABBAR *ir-ri-šu-š*]*u* / [KUG.BABBAR *i-na-din-š*]*u*.

Notes

4: for a similar verbal form cf. PBS 11/1, 40 (P228991) o.i. 4 (a model contract recorded in a Type II tablet) and BIN 7 205: 5 (dated to Samsu-iluna 7; cf. Kraus 1951: 53 fn. 17; Skaist 1994: 52 fn. 66); see also CAD Ḫ *s.v.* *ḫabātu* B, p. 11, "to borrow", and Dole 1965: 2–3. For the *ḫubuttatum*/eš-de$_2$-a loans see Skaist 1994: 52–56.
5: for the reading udru^{duru5} for the month name usually read ziz$_2$-a, see Englund 2011 and Cohen 1993: 118–119.

§5 (r.i'. 25–ii'. 12) Silver loan

r.i'.	25.	**1.**	16$^{!}$ ⌜$^{2}/_{3}$$^{?}$⌝ g[iĝ$_4$ kug-babbar]
	26.	**2.**	maš$_2$ 10 giĝ$_4$ ku[g-babbar]
	27.	**3.**	igi 3-⌜ĝal$_2$⌝ [...]
r.ii'.	1.	**4.**	t[aḫ-ḫe]-dam
	2.	**5.**	[ki...]-^{d}⌜EN⌝.ZU-ta
	3.	**6.**	[⌜x]-^{d}da-mu-ke$_4$
	4.	**7.**	⌜iti⌝ ab-e$_3$
	5.	**8.**	ud 17 zal-⌜la⌝-ta
	6.	**9.**	⌜kug⌝-bi i$_3$-la$_2$-e
	7.	**10.**	[t]ukum([Š]U.ĜAR.TUR.LAL)-bi
	8.	**11.**	[iti a]b-⌜e$_3$⌝
	9.	**12.**	[ud 17] zal:la-ta
	10.	**13.**	[kug-b]i la-ba-an-la$_2$
	11.	**14.**	[mu-DU] ⌜ud⌝ buru$_{14}$-ka
	12.	**15.**	[maš$_2$-bi b]i$_2$-⌜ib⌝-taḫ-e

"^{6}[...]-Damu (has received) ^{5}from [...]-Sîn $^{1–4}$16$^{!}$ $^{2}/_{3}$ she[kels of silver] – an interest rate of ... (of shekel) per 10 shekels of sil[ver] is to be ad[ded]; $^{7–9}$he will pay back that silver by the 17th day of the tenth month. $^{10–13}$If he does not pay back th[at silver] by the [17th day] of the ten[th month], $^{14–15}$he will add [its interest at the delivery] of the harvest".

Notes

2–3: despite being fragmentary, this interest formula seems to be different from the standard one listed in Ai II i 42 (maš$_2$ 10 giĝ$_4$ 2 giĝ$_4$-ta-am$_3$); unfortunately, it is not possible to provide a parallel case which can help to restore it.
14–15: these lines seem to express a penalty fee due to the delay in the returning of the silver loan. In fact, if the debtor is not able to pay back the silver by the 17th day of the tenth month, he will also have to add an interest rate (the entity of which is not entirely clear) at the delivery of the harvest. For a discussion about the possibility to relate the "harvest formula" to any specific calendar day or month, see Skaist 1994: 152–154. According to several assyriologists, in loan contracts the harvest formula would correspond to the third month in the Nippur calendar (iti šeg$_{12}$-a).[83]

---

[83] A silver loan contract from Kisurra (SANTAG 9, 145 = Goddeeris 2009: 179) is to be added to the two loan texts offered in Skaist 1994 as textual support to the equation "harvest time = third month".

§6 (r.ii’. 13–27) Silver loan

r.ii’.	13.	**1.**	[x] $^1/_2$ giĝ$_4$ kug-babbar
	14.	**2.**	[...] ⸢a$_2$⸣ iti-da
	15.	**3.**	[... igi x]-⸢ĝal$_2$ kug-babbar-ta⸣-am$_3$
	16.	**4.**	[taḫ]-ḫe-dam
	17.	**5.**	k[i] ⸢x-ib$_2$⸣-ĝar-ra-ka
	18.	**6.**	[^{Id}E]N.ZU-ma-an-šum$_2$-ke$_4$
	19.	**7.**	[šu ba]-an-ti
	20.	**8.**	[iti du$_6$-kug] ⸢ud⸣ 30-še$_3$
	21.	**9.**	[kug]-⸢bi i$_3$⸣-la$_2$-e
	22.	**10.**	[tu]kum([ŠU.ĜAR].TUR.LAL)-⸢bi⸣
	23.	**11.**	[iti du$_6$]-kug ud 30-še$_3$ kug-bi / la-ba-la$_2$
	24.	**12.**	[mu-D]U ud buru$_{14}$-<<ki>>-ka
	25.	**13.**	[šak]anka([KI.L]AM) nibru^{ki}-ka
	26.	**14.**	[a]l-du$^!$-a-gin$_7$
	27.	**15.**	[...] ⸢x⸣ kar$^?$

“$^{6–7}$[S]în-manšum has rece[ived] ^{5}from PN $^{1–4}$[x] $^1/_2$ shekels of silver [...] (its) monthly rent – [an interest rate of ...] of silver is to be added; $^{8–9}$he will pay back that [silver] by the 30th day [of the seventh month]. $^{10–11}$If he does not pay back that silver by the 30th day of the se[venth month], $^{12–14}$at the de[livery] of the harvest, according to the rate of exchange which is effective in Nippur ...”.

Notes

12 and **13**: in these two lines the KI-sign appears twice; while in line 12 it is to be deleted, having been wrongly inserted by the scribe, in line 13 it seems to have been added at a later time and therefore written in small handwriting.

13–14: for a discussion about the rate of exchange clause in loan contracts see Skaist 1994: 192–195.[84]

[84] See also another model contract (Spada 2011 §20), and references in Ai II iii 30–31.

6.

Museum n°: HS 1608 + HS 2629
Plates: 10–11 and 26–27
Measurements: 19.5×13.4×4 cm
State of preservation: the tablet is quite well preserved, except for the lower left and upper right corners, which are broken.

On the left column of the obverse (written by the teacher) there is a collection of four barley loan contracts, arranged on an ascending progression in the quantities of barley lent out, which differ from one another in regard to the interest clauses. Apparently, they belong to a longer collection of loan contracts, which is partially preserved in three fragmentary tablets: N 1326 (Type I tablet; it records the first part of §1, nearly all §3 and the first line of §4), CBS 10288 (Type I tablet; §3 and the first two lines of §4) and A 30173 (Type II tablet; §3, with some slight differences in the personal names and in the interest clause, followed by the first line of §4, which is here a catchline). It is these three tablets which have allowed us to restore the amount of barley in §3 and §4.
As usual in Type II tablets from Nippur, the right-hand columns appear to have been erased in order to be re-used by pupils copying the model on the left. On the reverse there is an extract from the acrographic list Nigga.

§1 (o.i. 1–9) Barley loan

o.i.	1.	**1.**	1(aš) 2(barig) 3(ban$_2$) ⸢še⸣ gur
	2.	**2.**	maš$_2$ 1(aš) gur 1(barig) 4(ban$_2$) še-ta-am$_3$
	3.	**3.**	sig$_9$-ge-de$_3$
	4.	**4.**	ki puzur$_4$-^{d}en-lil$_2$-ta
	5.	**5.**	^{I}dug$_3$-kar-^{d}en-lil$_2$-ke$_4$
	6.	**6.**	šu ba-an-ti
	7.	**7.**	⸢iti⸣ udru^{duru5}-ka
	8.	**8.**	[š]e u$_3$ maš$_2$-bi šum$_2$-mu-dam
	9.	**9.**	lu$_2$-ki-inim-ma iti-bi mu-bi-im

“$^{5–6}$Ṭāb-eṭēr-Enlil has received ^{4}from Puzur-Enlil $^{1–3}$1 *gur* 2 *barig* 3 *ban* (= 450 *sila*) of barley – an interest rate of 1 *barig* 4 *ban* (= 100 *sila*) of barley per 1 *gur* is to be charged; $^{7–8}$[the bar]ley with its interest is to be given back in the eleventh month. ^{9}(Its) witnesses, its month its year”.

Notes
3: for the expression sig$_9$-ge$_4$-de$_3$ in loan contracts see the commentary to **4** §1: 3.
5: for this personal name cf. Stol 1991: 192–193 and fn. 11.

§2 (o.i. 10–20) Barley loan

o.i.	10.	**1.**	2(aš) še gur
	11.	**2.**	maš$_2$ nu-ub-tuku
	12.	**3.**	⸢ki lu$_2$⸣-diĝir-ra-ta
	13.	**4.**	⸢^{I}*i$_3$*⸣-*li$_2$-ba-ni-i*-ke$_4$
	14.	**5.**	[š]u ba-an-ti
	15.	**6.**	iti-da ud-da 30-a
	16.	**7.**	gur-ru-dam

17. **8.** tukum-⸢bi⸣ iti-da ud-da 30-a
18. **9.** ⸢la⸣-ba-an-gur
19. **10.** ⸢maš$_2$⸣ 1(aš) gur 1(barig) 4(ban$_2$) ⸢še⸣-ta-am$_3$
20. **11.** [bi$_2$-ib-ta]ḫ-e

"$^{4-5}$Ilī-bānī has received ^{3}from Ludingira $^{1-2}$2 *gur* of barley (= 600 *sila*), without interest; $^{6-7}$it is to be returned by the 30th day of the month. $^{8-9}$If by the 30th day of the month he has not returned it, $^{10-11}$he will [add] an interest of 1 *barig* 4 *ban* (= 100 *sila*) of barley per 1 *gur*".

§3 (o.i. 21–31) Barley loan

o.i. 21. **1.** [3(aš)] še gur
22. **2.** [še$^{?}$ sila$^{?}$-a ĝ]al$_2$-la-a-še$_3$
23. **3.** [ki x]-^{d}*adad*-ta
24. **4.** [^{I}*i$_3$-li$_2$-e*]*n-nam*-ke$_4$
25. **5.** [šu ba]-⸢an⸣-ti
26. **6.** [ki uludin-b]i-še$_3$
27. **7.** [gur-r]u-dam
28. **8.** [tuku]m([ŠU.ĜAR.TUR].LAL)-bi
29. **9.** [ki uludin-b]i-še$_3$
30. **10.** [la-ba-an]-gur
31. **11.** [še maš$_2$ ĝa$_2$]-⸢ĝa$_2$⸣-dam

"$^{4-5}$[Ilī-e]nnam has rec[eived] ^{3}from [...]-Adad $^{1-2}$[3] *gur* of barley (= 900 *sila*), [as barley that] is not yet [in hand (lit: in the street)]; $^{6-7}$it is to [be returned] at it[s due-time]. $^{8-11}$If at it[s due-time he has not] returned it, [the barley (and its) interest] are to be paid".

Notes

2: this expression, frequently attested in the Ur III documents, is equated to the Akkadian *babtu*, "merchandise outstanding", i.e., not at hand at the time of the accounting, but the delivery of which is expected with certainty in the near future (CAD B, *s.v.* *babtu* 2, esp. a, with previous literature). Cf. also Englund 1990: 41 fn. 142 and Sigrist 1992: 112.
6 and **9**: for an analysis of the use of this expression see Roth 1979: 79 and 287–303; see also Charpin 1986: 480. This formula appears in Ai I i 1, 3, 5, 8, 11, 13, 15, Ura 1 235–236 and in several model contracts (cf. OBMC).

§4 (o.i. 32–36) Barley loan

o.i. 32. **1.** [3(aš) 2 (barig) 3(ban$_2$)] še gur
33. **2.** [... ki ...]-⸢x⸣-DU.SUM$^{?}$-ta
34. **3.** [... šu] ba-an-ti
35. **4.** [... gur]-ru-dam
36. **5.** [lu$_2$-ki-inim-ma iti-bi] ⸢mu⸣-bi-im

"^{3}[PN$_2$ has] received ^{2}from PN$_1$ ^{1}[3] *gur* [2 *barig* 3 *ban*] (= 1050 *sila*) of barley; ^{4}to be [returned in ...]. ^{5}[(Its) witnesses, its month], its year".

Duplicates:

N 1326 (r.i. 7’–11’ and r.ii. 1’–9’)

r.i.	7’.	**1.**	1(aš) 2(barig) 3(ban$_2$) še gur	
	8’.	**2.**	maš$_2$ 1(aš) gur 1(barig) 4(ban$_2$) še-ta-[am$_3$]	
	9’.	**3.**	sig$_9$-ge$_4$-de$_3$	§1
	10’.	**4.**	ki puzur$_4$-^{d}en-lil$_2$-t[a]	
	11’.	**5.**	^{I}⸢dug$_3$⸣-kar-^{d}en-lil$_2$-k[e$_4$]	
			rest of column missing	
r.ii.			[...]	
	1’.	**4.**	[^{I}*i*$_3$]-⸢*li*$_2$-*en-nam*-ke$_4$⸣	
	2’.	**5.**	[šu] ba-an-ti	
	3’.	**6.**	[ki] uludin-bi-še$_3$	
	4’.	**7.**	[g]ur-ru-dam	§3
	5’.	**8.**	[t]ukum([ŠU].ĜAR.TUR.LAL)-bi	
	6’.	**9.**	[ki] uludin-bi-še$_3$	
	7’.	**10.**	[l]a-ba-an-gur	
	8’.	**11.**	[še] maš$_2$ ĝa$_2$-ĝa$_2$-dam	
			double ruling	
	9’.	**1.**	[3(aš) 2(barig)] ⸢3(ban$_2$)⸣ še gur	§4
			rest of column missing	

CBS 10288 (o.ii’. 1’–7’ and o.ii’. 8’–10’)

o.ii’.			[...]	
	1’.	**5.**	šu ⸢ba-an⸣-[ti]	
	2’.	**6.**	ki uludin-⸢bi⸣-[še$_3$]	
	3’.	**7.**	gur-ru-dam	
	4’.	**8.**	tukum-bi	§3
	5’.	**9.**	ki uludin-bi-še$_3$	
	6’.	**10.**	la-ba-an-gur	
	7’.	**11.**	še maš$_2$ ĝa$_2$-ĝa$_2$-dam	
			double ruling	
	8’.	**1.**	3(aš) 2(barig) 3(ban$_2$) še ⸢gur⸣	
	9’.	**2.**	maš$_2$-bi [...]	§4
	10’.	**3.**	⸢x⸣ [...]	
			rest of column missing	

A 30173 (o.i. 1–11 and o.i. 12)

o.i.	1.	**1.**	3(aš) še gur	
	2.	**2.**	maš$_2$ nu-ub-tuku	
	3.	**3.**	ki lugal-ban$_3$-da-ta	
	4.	**4.**	^{I}*a-pil-*⸢*i*$_3$⸣*-li*$_2$*-šu*-ke$_4$	
	5.	**5.**	šu ba-an-ti	
	6.	**6.**	ki uludin-bi-še$_3$	§3
	7.	**7.**	gur-ru-dam	
	8.	**8.**	tukum-bi	
	9.	**9.**	ki uludin-bi-še$_3$	

10. **10.** la-ba-an-gur
11. **11.** še maš$_2$ ĝa$_2$-ĝa$_2$-dam

12. **1.** 3(aš) ⸢2(barig) 3(ban$_2$)⸣ še gur **§4**

The four columns of the reverse, almost completely preserved, contain an extract of the acrographic list Nigga, which is known from dozens of exemplars from Nippur, but poorly attested elsewhere. Moreover, there is no evidence that a standard series based on Nigga existed after the Old Babylonian period; instead, sections of Nigga were integrated into Izi and Kagal. The bold numbers refer to the corresponding lines in the standard OB Nigga series.[85]

r.i.			*three lines missing*
	4.		niĝ$_2$ ⸢x⸣ [...]
	5.	**5.**	niĝ$_2$-er[im$_2$](⸢NE⸣.[RU])
	6.	**6.**	niĝ$_2$-⸢a$_2$-zig$_3$$^{?}$⸣
	7.	**7.**	niĝ$_2$-a$_2$-⸢tak$_4$-a$^{!}$⸣
	8.	**8.**	niĝ$_2$-šu-tak$_4$-a
	9.	**9.**	niĝ$_2$-gig
	10.	**10.**	niĝ$_2$-al-di
	11.	**11.**	niĝ$_2$-sir$_3$-re
	12.	**12.**	niĝ$_2$-keš$_2$
	13.	**13.**	niĝ$_2$-keš$_2$
	14.	**14.**	niĝ$_2$-keš$_2$
	15.	**15.**	niĝ$_2$-keš$_2$
	16.	**16.**	niĝ$_2$-keš$_2$
	17.	**17.**	niĝ$_2$-dara$_2$
	18.	**18.**	niĝ$_2$-n[a]
	19.		niĝ$_2$ [...]
	20.		niĝ$_2$ [...]
	21.		⸢niĝ$_2$⸣ [...]
			2 lines broken
r.ii.	1.		⸢niĝ$_2$⸣ [...]
	2.		niĝ$_2$ ⸢x-x⸣
	3.	**26.**	niĝ$_2$ gibil
	4.	**27.**	niĝ$_2$ sumun
	5.	**28.**	niĝ$_2$ gul$^{!}$(U$_3$)-la
	6.		niĝ$_2$ ud-⸢su$_3$⸣-ra$_2$
	7.	**30.**	niĝ$_2$ ud-bi-ta
	8.	**29.**	niĝ$_2$ ⸢ud⸣-[ri]-a
	9.	**31.**	niĝ$_2$ ud ul-li$_2$-a
	10.	**32.**	niĝ$_2$-izi-la$_2$
	11.	**33.**	niĝ$_2$-gig-ga
	12.	**35.**	niĝ$_2$-kas$_7$
	13.	**36.**	niĝ$_2$-kas$_7$ ka-la$_2$
	14.	**37.**	niĝ$_2$ kum$_2$
	15.	**38.**	niĝ$_2$ te-en
	16.	**39.**	niĝ$_2$-ba sumun
	17.		niĝ$_2$ u$_2$-sumun
	18.		niĝ$_2$-gu$_7$ ak
	19.		niĝ$_2$-gu$_7$ ⸢x⸣
	20.	**44.**	niĝ$_2$ ⸢uš$_7$$^{?}$⸣-[ri-a]
			one line broken

85 For the edition of the OB Nippur Nigga cf. MSL 13, pp. 91–112 and DCCLT (http://oracc.org/dcclt/Q000052).

r.iii.	1.		⸢niĝ$_2$ x-x⸣
	2.	**47.**	niĝ$_2$-sur-ra
	3.	**48.**	niĝ$_2$-sur$_3^!$(ḪI×BAD)-ra
	4.	**50.**	kadra
	5.	**51.**	niĝ$_2$-dirig-ga
	6.	**52.**	niĝ$_2$-dirig-ga
	7.	**64.**	niĝ$_2$-silaĝ-ĝa$_2$
	8.	**54.**	niĝ$_2$-nam
	9.	**55.**	niĝ$_2$-nam-me
	10.	**65.**	niĝ$_2$-u$_2$-rum
	11.	**65.**	niĝ$_2$-⸢u$_2$⸣-rum
	12.	**65.**	niĝ$_2$-u$_2$-⸢rum$^?$⸣
	13.	**58.**	niĝ$_2$-kur$_2$ dug$_4$-dug$_4$
	14.	**59.**	niĝ$_2$-kur$_2$ di
	15.	**60.**	niĝ$_2$-lul
	16.	**61.**	niĝ$_2$-gi-na
	17.	**62.**	niĝ$_2$-zid
	18.	**67.**	niĝ$_2$-si-sa$_2$
	19.	**68.**	niĝ$_2$-si-sa$_2$
	20.	**92.**	niĝ$_2$ zal-la
	21.	**93.**	niĝ$_2$ zal-la
	22.	**69.**	niĝ$_2$-ĝal$_2$-⸢la⸣
r.iv.	1.	**70.**	[niĝ$_2$-ĝal$_2$]-⸢la⸣
	2.	**71.**	[niĝ$_2$-ĝal$_2$]-la
	3.		[niĝ$_2$-ĝa]l$_2^?$-la
	4.		[niĝ$_2$ x] kid$^?$
	5.		[niĝ$_2$] ⸢x⸣-ra$^?$
	6.	**76.**	[niĝ$_2$] ku$_4$-ku$_4$
	7.	**77.**	[ni]ĝ$_2$ e$_3$
	8.	**78.**	niĝ$_2$-⸢šam$_2$⸣-ma
	9.	**79.**	niĝ$_2$ šakanka(KI.LAM)
	10.	**80.**	niĝ$_2$ dug$_3$-ga
	11.	**81.**	niĝ$_2$ nu-dug$_3$-ga
	12.	**86.**	niĝ$_2$ sed$_x$(MUŠ$_3$-g.DI)
	13.	**83.**	niĝ$_2$ de$_6$-de$_6$
	14.	**84.**	niĝ$_2$-ba ĝar
	15.	**87.**	niĝ$_2$ mu tuku
	16.	**88.**	niĝ$_2$ a-na mu še$_{21}$-/a$^?$
	17.	**89.**	niĝ$_2$-mu-pad$_3$-da
	18.	**90.**	niĝ$_2$-ki-sa-ḫa
	19.	**91.**	niĝ$_2$-sa-ḫa
	20.	**96.**	⸢niĝ$_2$⸣-tuku
	21.	**97.**	[niĝ$_2$]-⸢nu⸣-tuku

7.

Museum n°: HS 1808
Plates: 12 and 28
Measurements: 5.6×5×2.7 cm
State of preservation: only the upper left corner is preserved.

On the obverse of this tablet only the first part of the loan contract written by the teacher occurs, whereas on the reverse, the two columns partially preserved record an extract from the Old Babylonian version of Izi.

o.i.	1.	**1.**	$^1/_2$ ma-na kug-babb[ar]
	2.	**2.**	ki *a-li*$_2$-DIĜIR-t[a]
	3.	**3.**	^{I}*i-din*-^{d}šakkan$_2$-k[e$_4$]
	4.	**4.**	[š]u ba-an-t[i]
	5.	**5.**	[ma]š$_2$-bi-še$_3$ 1 s[aĝ-munus]
	6.	**6.**	[gem]e$_2$-⸢^{d}⸣ša[kkan$_2$] m[u-ni-im]
			broken

"[3–4]Iddin-Šakkan has received [2]from Ali-ilum [1]half a mina of silver; [5–6]as its [inter]est a w[oman], na[med Ama]t-Šak[kan], (who is the slave-girl of Iddin-Šakkan, will serve as a pledge) ...".

Notes
The last line of this (partial) loan contract, in which a woman is given as antichretic pledge,[86] is restored here on the basis of three duplicates (with slight differences) of this model contract: the first one (Ist Ni 10108, Type II tablet) was published by Christine Proust (2007: 352), whereas the other two are recorded on two unpublished Type I tablets (CBS 10311, o.ii'. 1'–8' and N 4567, o.i. 1'–8'). Another copy appears in a fragmentary Type I or II tablet, UM 29-16-482.

Duplicates:

Ist Ni 10108 (o.i. 1–8) (= Proust 2007: 352)

o.i.	1.	**1.**	8 giĝ$_4$ kug-bab[bar]
	2.	**2.**	ki *a-li*$_2$-DIĜIR-ta
	3.	**3.**	^{I}*i-din*-^{d}šakkan$_2$-ke$_4$
	4.	**4.**	šu ba-an-ti
	5.	**5.**	[ma]š$_2$-bi-še$_3$ 1 saĝ-munus
	6.	**6.**	[*a*]-*ma-at*-^{d}šakkan$_2$
	7.	**7.**	[mu]-ni-im
	8.	**8.**	[gem]e$_2$ ⸢*i-din*⸣-^{d}šakkan$_2$
			rest of column missing

Notes
1: here (and probably in UM 29-16-482 o.ii'. 1) the amount of silver lent is much lower than that in the HS text.

[86] For a brief discussion on the loan contracts with antichretic pledge see the commentary to **4** §18: 9.

CBS 10311 (o.ii’. 1’–9’)

o.ii’.	1’.	**4.**	š[u ba-an-ti]
	2’.	**5.**	maš$_2$-bi-še$_3$ 1 s[aĝ-munus]
	3’.	**6.**	^{I}*a-ma-at-*^{d}EN.Z[U]
	4’.	**7.**	mu-ni-i[m]
	5’.	**8.**	geme$_2$ *i-din-*^{d}šakkan$_2$
	6’.	**9.**	^{I}*i-din-*^{d}šakkan$_2$ lugal-a-ni$^{!}$(IR)
	7’.	**10.**	^{I}*a-li*$_2$-DIĜIR-ra
	8’.	**11.**	kug-ta gub-ba-aš
	9’.	**12.**	⸢ib$_2$⸣-ta-⸢gub⸣-[bu]
			rest of column missing

Notes

6: apparently the name of the slave-girl pledged is slightly different from the other texts.

N 4567 (o.i. 1–8)

o.i.	1.	**1.**	[... kug-babba]r
	2.	**2.**	[ki *a-li*$_2$-DIĜIR]-⸢ta⸣
	3.	**3.**	^{I}⸢*i*⸣-*din-*^{d}šakkan$_2$ / lu$_2$-ĝi$_6$-a-du-du-ke$_4$
	4.	**4.**	šu ba-an-ti
	5.	**5.**	maš$_2$-bi-še$_3$
	6.	**6.**	1 saĝ-munus
	7.	**7.**	geme$_2$-^{d}[šakkan$_2$] m[u-ni-im]
	8.	**8.**	gem[e$_2$ *i-di*]*n*-⸢^{d}⸣[šakkan$_2$]
			rest of column missing

Notes

3: Iddin-Šakkan, the creditor, here is said to be a “night-watchman” (Sumerian luĝiadudu, Akkadian *ḫā’iṭu*).

UM 29-16-482 (o.ii’. 1–5)

o.ii’.	1.	**1.**	⸢8$^{?}$ giĝ$_4$⸣ kug-babbar
	2.	**2.**	ki *a-li*$_2$-DIĜIR-ta
	3.	**3.**	^{I}*i-din-*^{d}šakkan$_2$
	4.	**4.**	⸢šu⸣ ba-an-t[i]
	5.	**5.**	[maš$_2$-bi]-⸢še$_3$⸣
			rest of column missing

Izi is the longest and the most frequently attested among the acrographic lists.[87] Its Old Babylonian version often utilizes thematic principles for organizing its material, in addition to the acrographic ones. As Niek Veldhuis remarks (Veldhuis 2014: 170–171), even if there does not seem to be one coherent overall plan to the organization of this composition, Izi seems to have had a stable and well-recognized identity in the Old Babylonian world (and also later).

r.i'.			*traces*
	1'.	**72.**	saĝ [...]
	2'.	**73.**	ub-l[i-a]
	3'.	**74.**	mi$_2$ ⸢dug$_4$⸣-[ga]
r.ii'.			*traces*
	1'.	**93.**	⸢ḫi-ḫi⸣
	2'.	**94.**	⸢ḫi$^?$⸣-ḫi
	3'.	**95.**	dub$_3$
	4'.	**96.**	dub$_3$ bad
	5'.	**97.**	⸢dub$_3$ MUŠ$_3$-g.⸣

[87] Izi, in all its versions (Old Babylonian, Middle Babylonian and First Millennium) was first edited in 1971 by M. Civil (MSL 13); for a new edition of Old Babylonian Izi see Crisostomo *forthcoming*. Cf. also the online edition in DCCLT (http://oracc.org/dcclt/Q000050).

8.

Museum n°: HS 1451
Plates: 12 and 28
Measurements: 7×5.1×3 cm
State of preservation: only the upper right corner of the obverse is preserved.

The obverse of the tablet records the first part of a lease of real estate belonging to a *nadītu* of Ninurta, whereas the reverse (in which the signs are scratched on the surface) contains an extract from the Old Babylonian Ura, table 5 (corresponding to late Ura 20–22), which lists geographical names and stars.[88]

o.i.	1.	**1.**	[x sar e$_2$] kislaḫ
	2.	**2.**	[da e$_2$] ⸢*ip-qu*$_2$⸣-^{d}en-lil$_2$
	3.	**3.**	[e$_2$ ni]n-ku$_3$-zu lukur ^{d}nin-urta / [du]mu-munus *a-li*$_2$-DIĜIR
	4.	**4.**	[ki ni]n-ku$_3$-⸢zu⸣
	5.	**5.**	[^{I}*im-g*]*ur*-^{d}EN.ZU-ke$_4$
	6.	**6.**	[nam-g]a-an-tuš-a
	7.	**7.**	⸢a$_2$⸣ mu-⸢u$_8$⸣-še$_3$
	8.	**8.**	[x] giĝ$_4$ kug-babbar
	9.	**9.**	[i]b$_2$-ta-an-e$_3$
	10.	**10.**	[lu$_2$]-⸢ki⸣-inim-ma
	11.	**11.**	[iti-bi] ⸢mu-bi-im⸣
			broken

"^{5}[Img]ur-Sîn ^{9}rented ^{6}in tenan[cy ^{4}from Ni]n-kuzu $^{1-3}$an empty [house plot of x *sar*, next to the house] of Ipqu-Enlil, [(which is) the house of Ni]n-kuzu, *nadītu* of Ninurta, [daugh]ter of Ali-ilum, $^{7-8}$at an annual rent of [x] shekels of silver. $^{10-11}$[(Its) wit]nesses, [its month], its year".

Notes

1: the general meaning of kislaḫ (KI.UD) is "empty, unoccupied ground (of built-up house plots and orchards)"; when used in connection with houses, it denotes specifically "empty ground (next to the house)", which was utilized for various domestic activities. In some instances, KI.UD may also describe the house's courtyard; and, when used in connection with orchards, it means "uncultivated land" (cf. Steinkeller 1989: 123; see also Ura 1 164–167 and CAD K *s.v. teriktu*, p. 354[89]).

3: for a study on the *nadītu* of Ninurta in Nippur, with a focus on the differences between the *nadītu* institutions of OB Nippur and Sippar, see Stone 1982; cf. also Harris 1963. For the evidence that in Nippur there were *nadītu* dedicated to other gods than the city god see Goddeeris 2016: 35, comm. to l. 12.

The seal impression of a certain Nin-kuzu, *nadītu* of Ninurta, appears in PBS 8/1 8, which records the exchange of an orchard plot by Nin-kuzu and her sons (cf. Stone 1982: 55–56, fn. 15).

[88] See Veldhuis 1997: 46–47 and Veldhuis 2014: 149–157 for the division of OB Ura. For an edition of Ura 5 see MSL 11, pp. 93–128 and DCCLT (http://oracc.org/dcclt/Q000042).

[89] Cf. also Stol 2010: 173.

6: the formula nam-ga-an-tuš-a (and its variants nam-ga-an-tuš-(u$_2$)-še$_3$ and nam-ga-an-tuš-u$_3$-de$_3$), typical of Nippur, specifies that a real estate is rented in order to live in it[90] (cf. Stol 1993–1995: 164b–165a). See also CAD A$_2$, *s.v.* *aššābūtu*, “tenancy (of a house)”.

[90] See PBS 8/1 90, PBS 13 53 and SAOC 44 14. This formula appears also in other unpublished model contracts from Nippur: CBS 13934 (P230624), N 6041+ (P229567), PBS 8/1 102 (P230718).

OB Ura 5, which includes names of fields, cities, rivers and stars, consists of three sections. The first (lines 1–160) enumerates Nippur field names and describes the Sumerian landscape, with marshes, irrigated plains and levees. The second (lines 161–328) comprises exclusively names of cities and villages, with a relatively complete catalogue of the toponyms known from the late third and early second millennium. Finally, the third section (lines 329–386) deals with watercourses, from the simple irrigation channel to the river and canal.
Numbers in bold represent the corresponding lines of the edition of OB Nippur Ura 5 in MSL 11: 93–128.

r.i'.			[...]
	1'.		⸢x⸣-[...]
	2'.	**228.**	⸢kar-gu$_2$$^{?}$⸣-[du$_8$-a^{ki}]
	3'.	**229.**	⸢nibru^{ki}⸣-[ki-dug$_3$^{ki}]
			2 lines erased
	6'.		⸢x-x⸣-[...]
	7'.		⸢ka$_2$⸣-^{d}⸢x⸣[...]
	8'.	**232.**	ka$_2$-^{d}lu$_2$-l[al$_3$^{ki}]
	9'.	**233.**	⸢ka$_2$⸣-diĝir-ra[^{ki}]
r.ii'.			[...]
	1'.		[...]-⸢x^{ki}⸣
	2'.	**250.**	[ku-pi-i]n^{ki}
	3'.	**251.**	[a-r]a-wa⸢^{ki}⸣
	4'.	**252.**	[za]-ab-⸢ša⸣-l[i$^{?ki}$]
	5'.	**253.**	ma$_2$-ga[n^{ki}]
	6'.	**254.**	[m]e-luḫ-ḫa^{k}[^{i}]
	7'.	**255.**	⸢maš⸣-gan$_2$[^{ki}]
	8'.	**256.**	⸢maš⸣-gan$_2$-⸢šabra^{ki}⸣
	9'.	**257.**	[ma]š-gan$_2$-bu-uš^{ki}

9.

Museum n°: HS 1607 + HS 2946
Plate: 13–14 and 29–30
Measurements: 17×10×4 cm
State of preservation: only the central part of this tablet is preserved.

The right-hand columns, which are separated here from the left column by a vertical line, are blank and show traces of erasure; the left column, written by the teacher, is damaged.
On the reverse there is an extract of OB Nippur Ea.[91]

o.i.			*unknown number of lines missing*
	1'.	**1'.**	[ud kur$_2$-še$_3$ lu$_2$-lu$_2$]-⸢ra$^?$⸣
	2'.	**2'.**	[nu-mu-un]-gi$_4$-gi$_4$-⸢de$_3$⸣
	3'.	**3'.**	[mu lugal]-bi teš$_2$-bi / [in]-pad$_3$-de$_3$-eš
	4'.	**4'.**	[^{I}lu$_2$]-diĝir-ra šeš-gal
	5'.	**5'.**	[u$_3^?$ ^{Id}E]N.ZU-uru$_4$ šeš-a-ni
	6'.	**6'.**	[iti-da] 3(ban$_2$) še-ta-am$_3$
	7'.	**7'.**	[...] ⸢zid$_2$⸣-gu-ta-am$_3$
	8'.	**8'.**	[mu-am$_3^?$ 2]+4 ma-na
	9'.	**9'.**	[siki$^?$-t]a-am$_3$
	10'.	**10'.**	[u$_3^?$ 1]+5(diš) sila$_3$
	11'.	**11'.**	[i$_3$-ĝeš-t]a-am$_3$
	12'.	**12'.**	[in-na(-ab)-kalag]-⸢e$^?$⸣-ne
	13.	**13'.**	[lu$_2$ nu-mu-na(-ab)-kalag-g]e
			rest of column missing

"... $^{3'}$each of them has sworn by [the name of the king] that, $^{1'-2'}$[in the future one will not] return against [the other]. $^{4'-5'}$[Lu]-diĝira, the elder brother [and$^?$ S]în-ēriš, his brother, $^{12'}$will [provide] (their father/mother/sister?) $^{6'-11'}$[a monthly ration] of 3 *ban* (= 30 litres) of barley, [x *sila*] of flour, [an annual ration] of 6$^?$ minas [of wool (and)] 6$^?$ *sila* [of oil. $^{13'}$The one who does not provi]de (him/her) ...".

Notes

The preserved portion of the contract seems to be the final part of a document recording a division of inheritance between two brothers. While the section describing the division is lost, the no-contest clause and its oath are preserved; then a supporting section follows. Unfortunatey the part mentioning the recipient of this allowance has not been preserved, but it must be either the father (or the mother) or the unmarried sister of the two brothers. For similar texts cf. Stol 1998: 71–78 (where the beneficiaries are the father or the mother) and 85–95 (where the beneficiary is an unmarried sister).

1'–2': the restoration of these two lines is based on similar formulas in Nippur documents.[92]

3': usually, the oath stands at the end of the contract; apparently there is not a double dividing line which separates two different contracts, and this leads to consider it as an oath midway into the contract.

[91] For the digital edition of this OB list see DCCLT (http://oracc.org/dcclt/Q000055).

[92] Cf. e.g. Goddeeris 2016 n. 68: 14'–15'.

For another similar oath midway into an agreement see the division of inheritance published in Stone – Owen 1991: 39–40 (= PBS 8/1 16), where the oath is followed by a support clause.[93] See also the oath midway into a model marriage contract in Spada 2011 §42: 32–33.
6'–12': these lines express the obligations of two brothers allegedly in favour of their father/mother or their unmarried sister. The allowance, which almost invariably consists of rations of barley, wool and oil, appears to include here also a quantity of flour (l. 7'). According to Stol (1998: 64) "a reasonable minimum subsistence level was 2 litres of barley per day, which means 720 litres per year". If the proposed restoration is correct, it seems that here the annual amount of barley is the half, i.e., 30 litres per month. For a table of annual allowances in the Old Babylonian period see Stol 1998: 64–66.
13': the clause here partly reconstructed establishes that whoever does not support his father, mother or sister, will not exercise his right to inheritance.[94]

[93] For a discussion on this text see Stol 1998: 71–72.
[94] This seems to be the rule in Nippur: cf. e.g. PBS 8/1 16, PBS 8/2 116 and Goddeeris 2016 n. 11.

The sign list Ea, the name of which derived from the initial entry in the first millennium version, explains the reading and meaning of simple Sumerian signs; its basic format is: item marker (single vertical)[95] – gloss – sign. The same sign may be repeated multiple times with different glosses.

r.i'.	1.	**506.**	¶	ka-aš$_2$	⸢DUšeššig⸣
	2.	**507.**	¶	⸢gi⸣-im	DUšeššig
	3.	**508.**	¶	⸢im⸣	DUšeššig
	4.	**509.**	¶	⸢gi-ri⸣-im	DUšeššig
	5.	**512.**	¶	su-u$_2$	DU:DU
	6.	**511.**	¶	⸢re-e⸣	DU:DU
	7.	**513.**	¶	la-⸢aḫ⸣	DU.DU
	8.	**514.**	¶	⸢la-la-aḫ⸣	DU.DU.DU.⸢DU⸣
	9.	**515.**	¶	sa$_3$-a	ŠA$_6$
	10.	**515a.**	¶	ḫu-ud	ŠA$_6$
	11.	**515b.**	¶	mi-eš-ni	ŠA$_6$
	12.	**516.**	¶	še-eš	ŠEŠ$_2$
	13.	**516a.**	¶	si$_4^{?}$-ki-in	ŠEŠ$_2$
	14.		¶	(*line erased*)	
	15.	**516b.**	¶	e-re-en	EREN
	16.	**516c.**	¶	ig	IG
	17.	**516d.**	¶	ĝa$_2$-al	IG
	18.	**518.**	¶	uš$_2$	U[Š]
	19.	**517.**	¶	mi-eš	[UŠ$^{?}$]
	20.		¶	⸢x-x⸣-[x]	[...]
	21.	**518e.**	¶	ki-še-[x$^{?}$]	[UŠ×X]
	22.		¶	⸢x⸣-[...]	[...]
r.ii'.	1.	**518g.**	[¶]	[uš]	APIN
	2.	**519.**	¶	⸢e⸣-ri$_2$-iš	APIN
	3.	**520.**	¶	en-⸢gar$_3$⸣	APIN
	4.	**521.**	¶	ab-si-in	APIN
	5.	**522.**	¶	u$_4$-⸢ru⸣	APIN
	6.	**523.**	¶	a-p[i-i]n	APIN
	7.	**524.**	¶	a	AK$^{!}$(APIN)
	8.	**525.**	¶	⸢na⸣	⸢AK⸣
	9.	**526.**	¶	⸢ša⸣-a	AK
	10.	**526b.**	¶	⸢ra$^{!}$(AK)⸣	AK
	11.	**527.**	¶	⸢ke$^{?}$⸣	AK
	12.	**528.**	¶	a-ka	AK
	13.	**529.**	¶	⸢me⸣-e	AK×ERIN$_2$
	14.	**530.**	¶	⸢gi-im⸣	DIM$_2$
	15.	**531.**	¶	⸢di⸣-im	DIM$_2$
	16.	**533.**	¶	ši-di$^{!}$(TA)-im	DIM$_2$
	17.	**535.**	¶	ta-a	TA
	18.	**536.**	¶	la-⸢al⸣	TA×ḪI
	19.	**537.**	¶	gan$_2$-si	TA×IR
	20.	**538.**	¶	i-ri	URU
	21.	**539.**	¶	⸢u$_2$-ru⸣	URU×KAR$_2$

[95] The single vertical is here represented with the paragraph sign (¶).

	22.	**540.**	¶	u$_{2}$-ru	URU×[A$^{?}$]
r.iii’.	1.		[¶]	[...]	[...]
	2.	**543.**	[¶]	[u$_{2}$-ru-še]-⸢eb$^{?}$⸣	URU×ḪA
	3.	**544.**	[¶]	⸢ši⸣-ig	URU×TU
	4.	**545.**	[¶]	gu-ru	URU×GU
	5.	**546.**	[¶]	u$_{4}$	URU×MIN
	6.	**547.**	[¶]	ĝeš-⸢gal⸣	URU×MIN
	7.	**548.**	[¶]	⸢un-ke-en⸣	URU$^{!}$×BAR
	8.	**548a.**	[¶]	si-li-ig	URU×IGI
	9.	**549.**	[¶]	[š]a-ki-⸢ir⸣	URU×GA
	10.	**550.**	[¶]	ba-an-⸢šur⸣	⸢URU×URUDA⸣
	11.	**551.**	[¶]	ra-a	RA
	12.	**552.**	[¶]	la-⸢ag⸣	⸢ŠID⸣
	13.	**553.**	[¶]	[t]u-ba	ŠID
	14.	**554.**	[¶]	⸢za⸣-an-da-ra	ŠID
	15.	**555.**	[¶]	[šu]-⸢dum⸣	ŠID
	16.	**556.**	[¶]	[a-k]a	ŠID
	17.	**557.**	[¶]	[sa-a]ĝ$_{2}$	ŠID
	18.	**558.**	[¶]	[ši-i]d	ŠID
	19.	**559.**	[¶]	[sa]ĝ-ĝa$_{2}$	ŠID
	20.	**560.**	[¶]	[si]-la	ŠID
	21.	**561.**	[¶]	[gu$_{4}$]-ud	ŠID
	22.	**562.**	[¶]	[um-bi-s]aĝ	ŠID
	23.		[¶]	[...]	KIŠ
	24.		[¶]	[...]	⸢KIŠ⸣
	25.		[¶]	[...]	⸢GIR$_{3}$⸣
	26.		[¶]	[...]	⸢GIR$_{3}$$^{?}$⸣

4. Unidentified type of tablets

10.

Museum n°: HS 1752
Plates: 15 and 31–32
Measurements: 9.8×6.8×3.7 cm
State of preservation: just the right middle part of the tablet is preserved.

Due to the presence of more than one column per face, it seems to be a Type I tablet, containing some legal cases. Whether they are real legal cases or model texts concerning judicial proceedings[96] is not easy to establish: the omission of witnesses and dates has always been considered the most prominent characteristic of a model contract (see the commentary to lines 16–17 in **1** §10 above), but there are school exercises that also have a list of witnesses.[97]

Apparently three partial cases have been preserved, although it is not excluded that the text on the reverse (§3) may be the final part of the legal case in o.ii'. (§2).

§1 (o.i'. 1'–9')

o.i'.			*unknown number of lines missing*
	1'.	**1'.**	[...] ⸢x⸣
	2'.	**2'.**	[...] UD
	3'.	**3'.**	[... ^{d}nan]na([ŠEŠ].KI)-me-ša$_4$
	4'.	**4'.**	[...]-ta$^?$ in-tuš-a
	5'.	**5'.**	[...]-ni / [še]š-a-ni
	6'.	**6'.**	[...] ⸢NE?⸣
	7'.	**7'.**	[...] ⸢x⸣
	8'.	**8'.**	[...] ⸢x⸣
	9'.	**9'.**	[...] ⸢x⸣
			rest of column missing

[96] The so-called "model court cases" (sometimes called also "literary legal decisions") are sample court settlements used to train the scribes in the form of the functional court records. For a brief description of this genre, with previous bibliography, see George 2009: 142–147; see also Neumann 2004.
[97] This is the case of MS 2341 (P251564), a prism collecting seventeen model contracts, all of them ending with a list of one-to-three witnesses (the last one is always the scribe), and the date. For the edition of this prism see fn. 11 above.

§2 (o.ii'. 1'–12')

o.ii'. *unknown number of lines missing*

1'. **1'.** ⌜x x NE$^{?}$⌝ [x]
2'. **2'.** bi$_2$-in-du[g$_4$]
3'. **3'.** di-⌜kud⌝-e-n[e]
4'. **4'.** lu$_2$-ki-inim-[m]a
5'. **5'.** inim dub-ba-ka-ni
6'. **6'.** i-ib$_2$-sar-r[a$^{?}$]-a
7'. **7'.** ⌜igi⌝-ne-⌜ne in⌝-ĝar-⌜re-eš-*ma*⌝
8'. **8'.** igi me-še$_3$-am$_3$-^{d}nanna ⌜x⌝
9'. **9'.** šeš ad-da-na-⌜še$_3$⌝
10'. **10'.** [ki]šib nam-ibila-na
11'. **11'.** in-na-an-tak$_4$ <<in-tak$_4$>>
12'. **12'.** ⌜kišib lu$_2$⌝-ki-inim-ma[(-bi)]
rest of column missing

"[...] $^{2'}$he declared. $^{7'}$They$^{!}$ appeared before $^{3'}$the judges (saying that) $^{5'–6'}$the witness had registered his declaration (lit: his wording of the tablet); $^{8'–9'}$before Mešeam-Nanna$^{?}$, the ..., the brother of his father, $^{10'–11'}$he$^{?}$ has drawn up for him a [do]cument concerning his position as heir. $^{12'}$The seal of the witnesses (has been impressed on it)".

Notes

2': following standard usage in legal documents, bi$_2$-in-dug$_4$ refers to a defendant's entire declaration before the court, especially when he takes an oath (see e.g. Falkenstein 1956: 63f. fn. 6).
3'–7': unfortunately, the first part of this text is broken and it is not easy to fully understand what is recorded in it; therefore the translation of these lines is to be considered as tentative.
7': in legal contexts, the compound verb igi ~ ĝar means "to appear in a court" and is equated to the Akkadian formula *pāni šakānu* (cf. CAD Š$_1$, *s.v. šakānu*, mng. 5a, p. 140).

§3 (r.i' 1'-13')

r.i'. *unknown number of lines missing*

1' **1'.** *traces*
2'. **2'.** [x] ⌜lu$_2$ x x⌝ [x]
3'. **3'.** ⌜u$_3$⌝ lu$_2$-ki-inim-ma-bi
4'. **4'.** nam-erim$_2$-bi
5'. **5'.** ⌜ba-an⌝-kud-ru-uš
6'. **6'.** di dab$_5$-⌜ba⌝
7'. **7'.** ^{I}šu-^{d}nin-⌜ĝir$_2$-su x$^{?}$⌝ /zabar-⌜dab$_5$⌝
8'. **8'.** ^{I}za-[...] / ⌜ša$_{13}$⌝-dub-⌜ba-tuš⌝-a
9'. **9'.** ^{I}AN.AN-*še*-⌜*me-a*⌝ / ⌜ra⌝-bi$_2$-si$_2$-ka$_3$-tum
10'. **10'.** ^{I}*a-ḫu-ni* di-[kud]
11'. **11'.** ^{I}KA-^{d}nin-urta ⌜di⌝-kud
12'. **12'.** di-kud-bi-me-⌜eš⌝
13'. **13'.** ⌜lu$_2$-ki-inim-ma⌝
rest of column missing

"[2'–5'] ... and the witnesses took an oath: [6'] case accepted for trial. [7'–12'] Šu-Ninĝirsu ...$^{?}$, the *zabardab*-official, Za-[...], the *šadubatuša*, Ilān-šemea, the *rabi sikkatim*, Aḫuni, the jud[ge], KA-Ninurta, the judge: they are the judges; the witnesses ...".

Notes

4'–5': in Nippur, the verbs of this oath formula are kud, "to cut", $šum_2$, "to give" and $ĝal_2$ "to exist, to place". For the etymology of nam-$erim_2$, see Edzard 1975; according to him, the distinction between the "mu-lugal oath" and the "nam-$erim_2$ oath", is one of "timing": the first one should be the promise of an action to be taken or avoided in the future, the second an asseveration regarding an action in the past. For a different view of these two types of oath see the unpublished dissertation of I. Yoda (1993), where the author shows that the distinction was rather one of jurisdiction: the "nam-$erim_2$ oath" invokes divine sanction (and tends to be employed in a process between a private individual and an official, such as a trial), the "mu-lugal oath" royal sanction. See also Sallaberger 2008.

6': for the compound verbal form di ~ dab_5, see Dombradi 1996: 318–320, §421–423.

8': for a discussion of the meaning of the title *rabi sikkatim*, which originally referred to the officer in charge of the city gates, see Kleinerman 2011: 116, Charpin 2008: 188 and Pientka-Hinz 2006.[98]

9': to the best of my knowledge, $ša_{13}$-dub-ba-tuš-a only appears in OB Nippur Lu 26 (cf. MSL 12, p. 34).

[98] For the plural form *rubbû sikkātim* (*ru-bu* si_2*-ka-tim*) cf. CUNES 48-12-146 (= Chambon – Guichard 2015: 33–34).

11.
Museum n°: HS 2916
Plate: 16 and 32
Measurements: 4.6×3×2.2 cm
State of preservation: only a small fragment.

Due to the minuscule size of this fragment, it is not possible to assign it to a Type in the classification of the school exercises.

§1 (1’–6’) Barley loan

1’.	**1’.**	^{I}[...]
2’.	**2’.**	šu ba-[an-ti]
3’.	**3’.**	⌜iti$^{?}$ du$_6$$^{?}$-kug$^{?}$⌝-[x]
4’.	**4’.**	⌜gur$^{?}$-ru$^{?}$⌝-d[am$^{?}$]
5’.	**5’.**	⌜lu$_2$$^{?}$⌝-ki-i[nim-ma]
6’.	**6’.**	⌜iti⌝-bi ⌜mu⌝-[bi]

$^{1’–2’}$PN$_1$ has received [from PN$_2$ x *gur* of barley]; $^{3’–4’}$to be returned in the seventh$^{?}$ month$^{?}$. $^{5’–6’}$[(Its) wit]nesses, its month, [its] year”.

Notes
3’–4’: even if the surface is badly preserved, we expect here the term for the repayment of the loan (probably a month name, or even the harvest formula), followed by the verb of repayment. The above transliteration is to be considered as tentative.

§2 (7’–9’) Barley loan

7’.	**1.**	5$^{?}$(aš) še [gur]
8’.	**2.**	maš$_2$ nu-ub-t[uku]
9’.	**3.**	ki l[u$_2$-...-ta]

“[PN$_1$ has received] ^{3}from L[u-...] $^{1–2}$5$^{?}$ [*gur*] of barley, without interest...”.

4. INDEXES

1. Personal names[99]

[99] In the indexes, all references to duplicates are followed in parentheses by the number of the text and section in which the duplicate’s edition is to be found in this book.

Lu-Dumuzida (lu$_2$-^{d}dumu-zi-da)

- **4** r.ii. 2’, 7’, 13’

Lu-gidgid (lu$_2$-gid$_2$-gid$_2$)

- **CBS 2298** o. 5 (**2** §2)

Lu-Isinna (lu$_2$-i$_3$-si-in^{ki}-na)

- **4** r.iv. 13’

Lu-Ninmarki (lu$_2$-nin-mar-ki)

- father of Lu-Nuska: **5** o.i. 4

Lu-Ninšubur (lu$_2$-^{d}nin-šubur)

- **MS 3176/5** r.i. 19, 24 (**3** §1)

Lu-Ninurta (lu$_2$-^{d}nin-urta)

- **CBS 8663+** o.i. 4’, 9’, r.i’. 3 (**3** §1); **Ist Ni 1576** o.i. 1’, 6’ (**3** §1); **UM 55-21-441** r.ii. 2’ (**3** §1)

Lu-Nuska (lu$_2$-^{d}nuska)

- son of Lu-Ninmarki: **5** o.i. 3, 11
- **4** o.ii. 9

Lu-ursaĝgalzu (lu$_2$-ur-saĝ-gal-zu)

- **4** r.iii. 21’, 22’

Lu-[...] (l[u$_2$-...])

- **11** 9’

Lugal-amaru (lugal-a-ma-ru)

- master of Ištar-ennam: **1** A.i. 2’, 4’, 10’; **CBS 1206** o.i’. 3’, 6’, 8’, 12’ (**1** §1); **CBS 8437** o. 3, r. 8, 11 (**1** §1); **MS 4979** o. 3, 4, 16, 18 (**1** §1); **N 950** o.i’. 3, 4 (**1** §1); **N 2469** o. 8’ (**1** §1); **N 4075** o.ii’. 1’, 7’ (**1** §1); **UM 29-15-617** o.ii’. 4, 5 (**1** §1)

Lugal-banda (lugal-ban$_3$-da)

- **A 30173** o.i. 3 (**6** §3)

LutilaDI (lu$_2$-ti-la-DI)

- simug: **1** B.i. 9; **CBS 13866** r.ii’. 13 (**1** §5); **N 5863** r.iii’. 14’ (**1** §5)

Mannum-balum-ilim (*ma-nu-um-ba-lu*-AN)

- **4** r.ii. 20’

Martu-ziĝu (^{d}mar-tu-zi-ĝu$_{10}$)

- **MS 3176/5** o.iii’. 3 (**4** §6)

Mešeam-Nanna (me-še$_3$-am$_3$-^{d}nanna)

- **10** o.ii’. 8’

Nanna-meša (^{d}nanna-me-ša$_4$)

- **1** C.ii. 10, 11, 20; **4** o.iii. 9; o.v. 5; **10** o.i’. 3’; **3N-T567** o.i. 6, 7, 14 (**1** §11)

Nanna-[...] (^{d}na[nna-...])

- **2** B.i. 5’

Nin-ḫeĝal (nin-ḫe$_2$-ĝal$_2$)

- wife of Ur-kuzu, mistress of DIĜIR-⸢x⸣-ma: **1** B.iii. 30, 35, C.i. 7, 11, 17; **MS 4979** r. 17 (**1** §9); **UM 55-21-333** o.i. 2’, 7’ (**1** §9)

Nin-kuzu (nin-ku$_3$-zu)

- lukur Ninurta and daughter of Ali-ilum: **8** o.i. 3, 4

Ninurta-palil (^{d}nin-urta-palil)

- master of Abum-waqar: **1** B.iii. 3, 4, 11, 13, 17; **CBS 8868** o.i. 1’, 9’, 10’, 14’ (**1** §8); **IM 58639** o.ii’. 2’, 3’, 9’ (**1** §8); **SLFN 74, 3N-T927, 513** ii’. 3’, 4’ (**1** §8)

Nuska-amaḫ (^{d}nuska-a$_2$-maḫ)

- father of Ur-dukuga: **4** r.v. 13’

Puzur-Enlil (puzur$_4$-^{d}en-lil$_2$)

- **6** o.i. 4; **N 1326** r.i. 10’ (**6** §1)

Puzur-Ninkarrak (puzur$_4$-^{d}nin-kar-ra-ak)

- master of Ilī-aj-abāš: **5** o.i. 5, 10

Sîn-ēriš (^{d}EN.ZU-uru$_4$)

- brother of Lu-diĝira: **9** o.i. 5’

Zibbat-Lamassi (*zi-ib-ba-at-*^{d}lamma)
- **4** r.iii. 23’

[...]-Adad ([...]-^{d}*adad*)
- **6** o.i. 23

[...]-Damu ([x]-^{d}da-mu)
- **5** r.ii’. 3

[...]-⸢x⸣-DU.SUM$^{?}$
- **6** o.i. 33

[...]-Sîn ([...]-^{d}EN.ZU)
- **5** r.ii’. 2

2. Deities

Nisaba

- ^{d}nisaba za$_3$-mi$_2$: **4** r.v. 14’

Nuska

→ as theophoric element in personal names:
  - Lu-Nuska
  - Nuska-amaḫ
  - Ur-Nuska

Pabilsaĝa

→ as theophoric element in the personal name:
  - Ur-Pabilsaĝa

Samana

→ as theophoric element in the personal name:
  - Ur-Samana

Sebetti

→ as theophoric element in the personal name:
  - Warad-Sebetti

Sîn

→ as theophoric element in personal names:
  - Awīl-Sîn
  - Imgur-Sîn
  - Sîn-ēriš
  - Sîn-iddinam
  - Sîn-manšum
  - Sîn-rēmēni
  - Sîn-šēmi
  - Ur-Sîn

Šakkan

→ as theophoric element in personal names:
  - Amat-Šakkan
  - Iddin-Šakkan

Šubula

→ as theophoric element in the personal name:
  - Ur-Šubula

Šulpa’e

→ as theophoric element in the personal name:
  - Ur-Šulpa’e

Utu/Šamaš

- niĝ$_2$-ŠID igi ^{d}utu-še$_3$: **4** r.ii. 26’

→ as theophoric element in personal names:
  - Amat-Šamaš
  - Šamaš-bāni
  - Utu-manšum

3. Toponyms

4. Glossary

Sumerian words

a_2 "wages, rent"

- a_2-bi: **1** C.i. 33
- a_2-bi-še$_3$: **1** C.ii. 24; **3N-T567** o.i. 18 (**1** §11)
- a_2-bi iti-da: **3N-T567** o.i. 11 (**1** §11); **CBS 8663+** o.i. 6' (**3** §1); **Ist Ni 1576** o.i. 3' (**3** §1); **MS 3176/5** r.i. 21 (**3** §1)
- a_2 iti-da: **5** r.ii'. 14
- a_2 mu-u$_2$-a-še$_3$: **1** C.i. 29
- a_2 mu-u$_8$-še$_3$: **8** o.i. 7
- a_2-ni-e: **5** o.i. 14
- a_2-ni-še$_3$: **1** C.iii. 22

a-na-me-a-bi "as many as there may be, everything"

- **1** A.i. 5', A.iii. x+11, B.ii. 29, B.iii. 14, C.i. 12; **CBS 1206** o.i'. 9' (**1** §1); **CBS 8437** r. 9 (**1** §1); **CBS 8868** o.i. 11' (**1** §8); **N 4075** o.ii'. 2' (**1** §1); **UM 55-21-333** o.i. 3' (**1** §9)

a-ra$_2$ "times"

- a-ra$_2$ 2-kam: **1** C.iii. 22

a-šag$_4$ "field"

- a-šag$_4$ NUMUN$_2$.ŠE$_3$: **4** r.iii. 18'
- kiĝ$_2$ a-šag$_4$-ga al-ak-e: **5** o.i. 15

a_2-tuku "surplus, profit"

- a_2-tuku ĝal$_2$-la-bi: **4** o.iv. 5, r.i. 8', 21'

abul "gate"

- abul-la-ta: **1** C.iii. 27

ad-da "father"

- ad-da til$_3$-la: **1** A.i. 11', A.ii. 9', B.ii. 1, 33, B.iii. 18, C.i. 16; **CBS 1206** o.i'. 13' (**1** §1); **CBS 8437** r. 11 (**1** §1); **CBS 8868** o.i. 14' (**1** §8); **N 4075** o.ii'. 8' (**1** §1); **UM 55-21-333** o.i. 6' (**1** §9)
- šeš ad-da-na: **10** o.ii'. 9'

aĝ$_2$ "to measure"

- al-aĝ$_2$-de$_3$: **4** r.ii. 8'
- al-aĝ$_2$-e: **1** C.ii. 21; **2** A.ii'. 10'; **3** A.ii'. 4', B.ii'. 7'; **4** r.ii. 16'; **3N-T567** o.i. 15 (**1** §11)
- la-ba-aĝ$_2$-e: **3** A.ii'. 8'

ama "mother"

- ama til$_3$-la: **1** A.iii. x+15

ama-ar-gi$_4$ ~ ĝar "to establish (one's) freedom"

- ama-ar-gi$_4$-ni in-ĝar: **1** A.ii. 19', A.iii. x+23, B.ii. 9, B.iii. 6; **CBS 8437** o. 4 (**1** §1); **CBS 8868** o.i. 2' (**1** §8), r.i'. 4' (**1** §5), r.ii'. 9' (**1** §7); **CBS 13866** r.ii' 6 (**1** §5); **IM 58639** o.ii'. 4' (**1** §8); **MS 4979** o. 6 (**1** §1); **N 950** o.i'. 5 (**1** §1); **N 5863** r.iii'. 5' (**1** §5); **SLFN 74, 3N-T927, 513** i'. 6' (**1** §7), ii'. 6'–7' (**1** §8); **UM 29-15-617** o.ii'. 6 (**1** §1)
- ama-ar-gi$_4$-ni in-ĝar-re-ne: **1** B.iii. 31–32

arad$_{(2)}$ "slave"

- arad$_2$-da-a-bi: **1** C.iii. 18, 29
- arad$_2$-da(-a)-ni: **1** D.i. 11 (-a); **5** o.i. 18
- **1** B.ii. 6 (arad$_2$), B.iii. 3 (arad$_2$), C.ii. 32 (arad$_2$); **5** o.i. 10 (arad$_2$); **CBS 8868** r.ii'. 6' (arad$_2$) (**1** §7); **IM 58639** o.ii'. 2' (**1** §8); **SLFN 74, 3N-T927, 513** i'. 4' (**1** §7), ii'. 3' (**1** §8)

ba "to divide into shares, to allot"

- i$_3$-ba-e-ne: **2** B.i. 3'; **4** o.iv. 7, r.i. 10', 23'
- in-na-an-ba: **CBS 8437** r. 5 (**1** §1)

^{ĝeš}banšur-zag-gu$_{(2)}$-la$_{(2)}$ "a cultic table"

- **CBS 8437** r. 2 (**1** §1); **MS 4979** o. 9 (-gu$_2$-la$_2$) (**1** §1); **N 2469** o. 2' (**1** §1)

buru$_{14}$ "harvest"

- mu-DU ud buru$_{14}$-ka: **5** r.i'. 2, r.ii'. 11, 24
- ud buru$_{14}$-(a-)ka: **4** o.ii. 12, 15; **CBS 2298** o. 9 (a-) (**2** §2)

burud$_x$ "to perforate"

- e$_2$-bi al-burud$_x$: **CBS 8663+** o.i. 19' (**3** §1); **MS 3176/5** r.i. 28 (**3** §1)

da "side"

- **1** B.i. 7; **4** r.iv. 18'; **8** o.i. 2; **CBS 13866** r.ii'. 12 (**1** §5); **N 5863** r.iii'. 12' (**1** §5)

dab$_5$ "seize"

- di dab$_5$-ba: **10** r.i'. 6'

dadag "to clean"

cf. saĝ-ki ~ dadag

dam "spouse"

- dam til$_3$-la: **1** C.i. 18; **UM 55-21-333** o.i. 7' (**1** §9)

dam-gar$_3$ "merchant"

- dam-gar$_3$-ra-ke$_4$-ne: **4** o.iv. 3

de$_2$ "to pour"

cf. u$_2$-gu ~ de$_2$

di "judicial case"

- di dab$_5$-ba: **10** r.i'. 6'

di-kud "judge"
- di-kud: **10** r.i'. 10', 11'
- di-kud-bi-me-eš: **10** r.i'. 12'
- di-kud-e-ne: **4** r.ii. 5'; **10** o.ii'. 3'

du "to go"
- al-du-a-gin_7: **5** r.ii'. 26

DU "to bring"
cf. mu-DU

dub "tablet"
- inim dub-ba-ka-ni: **10** o.ii'. 5'

dub-sar "scribe"
- dub-sar tur: **4** r.v. 12'

dug ~ gaz "to break the pot (of slavery)"
- dug nam-$arad_2$-da-ni in-gaz: **CBS 8868** o.i. 4' (**1** §8)
- dug nam-$geme_2$-ni-$še_3$ in-gaz: **1** A.iii. 2–3, B.i. 2–3; **CBS 8437** o. 6–7 (**1** §1); **CBS 8868** r.i'. 6'–7' (**1** §5); **CBS 13866** r.ii'. 8 (**1** §5); **N 950** o.i'. 7 (**1** §1); **N 5863** r.ii'. 2'–3' (**1** §4), r.iii'. 7'–8' (**1** §5); **UM 29-15-617** o.ii'. 8–9 (**1** §1)

dug_3 "to make/be good"
cf. $šag_4$ ~ dug_3

dug_4 "to say, to speak"
- bi_2-in-dug_4: **10** o.ii'. 2'

dumu "son"
- **1** A.ii. 16', B.iii. 22, C.i. 26, D.ii. 17'; **4** o.iii. 10, r.v. 13'; **5** o.i. 4; **MS 4979** r. 3 (**1** §9)

dumu-munus "daughter"
- **8** o.i. 3

/e/ "to say, to speak"
- al-la-be_2-a: **5** r.i'. 11
- in-na-an-ne-eš: **4** r.ii. 9'

e_2 "house"
- e_2-a-ni-$še_3$: **4** r.iv. 22'
- e_2-bi: **CBS 8663+** o.i. 19' (**3** §1); **MS 3176/5** r.i. 28 (**3** §1)
- e_2 kislaḫ: **8** o.i. 1
- e_2 UŠ.UŠ: **CBS 8663+** o.i. 2' (**3** §1)
- lugal e_2-a(-ke_4): **4** r.ii. 14' (-ke_4); **CBS 8663+** r.i'. 2 (**3** §1); **MS 3176/5** r.i. 32 (**3** §1)
- ur_2 e_2-a: **4** r.iii. 13'
- ur_3 e_2-a: **4** r.iii. 15'

^{ĝeš}gi-muš "punting pole"
- **1** C.i. 23, C.ii. 7; **3N-T567** o.i. 3 (**1** §11)

gi-na "properly"
- **4** r.ii. 29'

gu_7 "to eat, to enjoy the usufruct"
- ba-an-gu_7: **4** r.ii. 3'
- mu še-bi in-gu_7-a-aš: **4** r.ii. 4'
- ninda an-ni-ib-gu_7-e: **1** C.iii. 13

gub "to stand"
  cf. igi ~ gub
- kug-ta gub-ba-aš ib_2-ta(-an)-gub-bu: **5** o.i. 12–13 (-an); **CBS 10311** o.ii'. 8'–9' (**7**)
- kug-ta ib_2-ta-gub: **4** r.iv. 20'

gudug "*pašīšum*-priest"
- gudug ^{d}nin-urta: **1** A.ii. 15'

gur "to return"
- gur-ru-dam: **1** C.ii. 2, 26; **6** o.i. 16, 27, 35; **11** 4'; **3N-T567** o.i. 20 (**1** §11); **A 30173** o.i. 7 (**6** §3); **CBS 10288** o.ii'. 3' (**6** §3); **N 1326** r.ii. 4' (**6** §3)
- gur-ru-de_3: **2** A.i'. 1', 5'
- la-ba-an-gur: **6** o.i. 18, 30; **A 30173** o.i. 10 (**6** §3); **CBS 10288** o.ii'. 6' (**6** §3); **N 1326** r.ii. 7' (**6** §3)

$ĝal_2$ "to be available"
- a_2-tuku $ĝal_2$-la-bi: **4** o.iv. 5, r.i. 8', 21'
- $niĝ_2$ gub-ba $ĝal_2$-la-bi: **4** r.ii. 28'
- sila-a $ĝal_2$-la-a-$še_3$: **6** o.i. 22

ĝar "to place"
  cf. ama-ar-gi_4 ~ ĝar
  cf. igi ~ ĝar
  cf. inim ~ ĝar
- $ĝa_2$-$ĝa_2$-dam: **4** o.ii. 17; **6** o.i. 31; **A 30173** o.i. 11 (**6** §3); **CBS 10288** o.ii'. 7' (**6** §3); **N 1326** r.ii. 8' (**6** §3)
- im-$ĝa_2$-$ĝa_2$: **4** r.iii. 15'
- in-ĝar-re-eš: **4** r.ii. 24'
- mu-un-ĝar-re-eš: **4** r.ii. 27'
- nu-$ĝa_2$-$ĝa_2$: **4** r.i. 18'

^{ĝeš}ĝisal "oar"
- **1** C.ii. 8; **3N-T567** o.i. 4 (**1** §11)

ĝiškim-ti "trust"
- ĝiškim-ti-$še_3$: **MS 3176/5** o.iii'. 2 (**4** §6)

- iti 4-kam: **4** r.iii. 4’

^{dug}kab$_2$-dug$_4$-ga “gauged measuring vessel”
- **4** r.iii. 5’

kalag “to provide for”
- in-na-ab-kalag-ge: **1** B.ii. 21; **N 5863** r.ii’. 14’ (**1** §4)
- in-na(-ab)-kalag-e$^?$-ne: **9** o.i. 12’
- nu-mu-na(-ab)-kalag-ge: **9** o.i. 13’

kar “harbour, quay”
- kar-bi-še$_3$: **1** C.ii. 1, 25
- kar nibru^{ki}-ka: **3** A.ii’. 3’, 7’
- kar nibru^{ki}-ta$^!$: **3N-T567** o.i. 19 (**1** §11)

kaš “beer”
- kaš sa$_{10}$-sa$_{10}$-de$_3$: **CBS 2298** o. 3, 10, 13 (**2** §2)

ki-la$_2$ “weight”
- kug pad-ra$_2$ ki-la$_2$: **MS 3176/5** o.iii’. 8 (**4** §6)

kiĝ$_2$ “work”
- kiĝ$_2$ a-šag$_4$-ga al-ak-e: **5** o.i. 15
- kiĝ$_2$ ak-de$_3$: **4** r.i. 13’
- kiĝ$_2$-bi: **4** r.i. 19’

kiĝ$_2$-gi$_4$-a “work”
- kiĝ$_2$-gi$_4$-a-še$_3$ al-DU: **5** o.i. 16

^{na4}kinkin zi-bi “*zību*-millstone”
- ^{na4}kinkin zi-bi šu si$_3$-ga: **CBS 1206** o.i’. 1’ (**1** §1); **CBS 8437** r. 1 (**1** §1); **MS 4979** o. 8 (**1** §1); **N 2469** o. 1’ (**1** §1)

^{ĝeš}kiri$_6$ “orchard”
- ^{ĝeš}kiri$_6$-še$_3$: **4** r.iv. 9’

kislaḫ “unbuilt plot”
- e$_2$ kislaḫ: **8** o.i. 1

kišib “sealed tablet, document; seal”
- gaba-ri kišib-ba-ni: **4** o.ii. 4, o.v. 12; **MS 3176/5** o.iii’. 42 (**4** §9)
- kišib-a-ni: **1** B.ii. 22
- kišib-bi: **4** o.ii. 2, o.v. 10; **CBS 8663+** o.i. 20’ (**3** §1); **MS 3176/5** o.iii’. 40 (**4** §9), r.i. 29 (**3** §1); **UM 29-13-408a** o.ii’. 11’ (**4** §9)
- kišib lu$_2$-ki-inim-ma: **10** o.ii’. 12’
- kišib nam-ibila-na: **10** o.ii’. 10’

la$_2$ "to pay, to weigh"
- i$_3$-la$_2$-e: **1** D.i. 16; **3** A.i'. 1'; **5** r.i'. 4, 18, r.ii'. 6, 21; **CBS 8663+** o.i. 11', 17' (**3** §1); **Ist Ni 1576** o.i. 8' (**3** §1); **MS 3176/5** r.i. 26 (**3** §1)
- in-na-an-la$_2$: **4** r.iii. 27', r.iv. 6'
- la-ba(-an)-la$_2$: **5** r.i'. 22 (-an), r.ii'. 10 (an), 23

laḫtan$_6$ "vat"
- laḫtan$_6$ MA$^?$: **4** r.iii. 6'
- laḫtan$_6$ TI LAM: **4** r.iii. 7'

lu$_2$ "man, person"
- lu$_2$-lu$_2$-ra: **9** o.i. 1'

lu$_2$-en-nu-uĝ$_3$ "guard"
- **1** C.iii 26, 30$^?$

lu$_2$-ĝi$_6$-a-du-du "night-watchman"
- **N 4567** o.i. 3

lu$_2$-ki-inim "witness"
- lu$_2$-ki-inim-ma(-bi): **1** C.ii. 3, 27, D.i. 17; **3** B.ii'. 8'; **4** o.i. 9, o.ii. 18, o.iii. 4, o.iv. 8, r.iii. 16', r.iv. 23', r.v. 9'; **6** o.i. 9, 36; **8** o.i. 10; **10** o.ii'. 4', 12', r.i'. 3' (-bi), 13'; **11** 5'

lu$_2$-kur$_2$ "foreigner, another man"
- lu$_2$-kur$_2$-še$_3$: **4** r.i. 19'

lu$_2$-na-me "someone, anyone"
- **1** D.i. 15$^?$

lugal "owner, master"
    cf. mu lugal ~ pad$_3$
- lugal-a-ni(-ir): **1** A.iii. x+22 (-ir), B.ii. 8 (-ir), B.iii. 5, 29, 34, C.i. 6, C.iii. 15; **CBS 8868** o.i. 1' (**1** §8), r.i'. 3' (**1** §5), r.ii'. 8' (**1** §7); **CBS 10311** o.ii'. 6' (**7**); **CBS 13866** r.ii'. 5 (**1** §5); **IM 58639** o.ii'. 3' (**1** §8); **MS 4979** o. 5 (-ir) (**1** §1), r. 16 (-ir) (**1** §9); **N 950** o.i'. 4 (**1** §1); **N 5863** r.iii'. 4' (**1** §5); **SLFN 74, 3N-T927, 513** i'. 5' (**1** §7), ii'. 5' (**1** §8); **UM 29-15-617** o.ii'. 5 (**1** §1)
- lugal e$_2$-a(-ke$_4$): **4** r.ii. 14' (-ke$_4$); **CBS 8663+** r.i'. 2 (**3** §1); **MS 3176/5** r.i. 32 (**3** §1)
- lugal še-še$_3$: **4** r.ii. 16'

lukur "a priestess"
- lukur ^{d}nin-urta: **8** o.i. 3

^{ĝeš}ma$_2$ "boat"
- ^{ĝeš}ma$_2$ 2(u)-gur: **1** C.i. 21
- ^{ĝeš}ma$_2$ 5(u)-gur: **1** C.ii. 5; **3N-T567** o.i. 1 (**1** §11)
- ^{ĝeš}ma$_2$ silim-ma: **1** C.i. 32, C.ii. 23; **3N-T567** o.i. 17 (**1** §11)
- **1** C.i. 25, C.ii. 10; **3N-T567** o.i. 6 (**1** §11)

- mu lugal-bi in-pad$_3$(-de$_3$)-eš: **1** C.i. 19–20 (-de$_3$); **MS 4979** r. 18 (**1** §9); **UM 55-21-333** o.i. 8’ (-de$_3$) (**1** §9)
- mu lugal-bi teš$_2$-bi in-pad$_3$-de$_3$-eš: **9** o.i. 3’

mu$_4$ “to clothe oneself”
- tug$_2$ an-ni-ib$_2$-mu$_4$-mu$_4$: **1** C.iii. 16, D.i. 9

mu-DU “delivery”
- mu-DU ud-buru$_{14}$-ka: **5** r.i’. 2, r.ii’. 11, 24

^{ĝeš}muru$_5$-za-nu-um “a type of table”
- **CBS 8437** r. 4 (**1** §1); **MS 4979** o. 11 (**1** §1); **N 2469** o. 4’ (**1** §1)

nam-arad$_{(2)}$ “status as a slave”
- nam-arad$_2$-da-ni: **CBS 8868** o.i. 4’ (**1** §8)
- nam-arad$_{(2)}$-da-ni-še$_3$: **1** B.i. 34, B.ii. 24, 30, B.iii. 15 (arad$_2$), C.i. 13 (arad$_2$); **CBS 8868** o.i. 12’ (arad$_2$) (**1** §8); **UM 55-21-333** o.i. 4’ (arad$_2$) (**1** §9)

nam-erim$_2$ “oath”
- nam-erim$_2$-bi: **10** r.i’. 4’

nam-geme$_2$ “status as a slave-girl”
- nam-geme$_2$-ni-še$_3$: **1** A.i. 7’, A.iii. 2, x+12, B.i. 2; **CBS 1206** o.i’. 10’ (**1** §1); **CBS 8437** o. 6, r. 9 (**1** §1); **CBS 8868** r.i’. 6’ (**1** §5); **CBS 13866** r.ii’. 8 (**1** §5); **MS 4979** o. 17 (-<ni>-) (**1** §1); **N 950** o.i’. 7 (**1** §1); **N 2469** o. 9’ (**1** §1); **N 4075** o.ii’. 4’ (**1** §1); **N 5863** r.ii’. 2’ (**1** §4), r.iii’. 7’ (**1** §5); **UM 29-15-617** o.ii’. 8 (**1** §1)

nam-sikil “purity; freedom”
- **1** A.iii. 4, B.i. 4; **CBS 8437** o. 8 (**1** §1); **CBS 8868** o.i. 5’ (**1** §8), r.i’. 8’ (**1** §5); **CBS 13866** r.ii’. 9 (**1** §5); **N 5863** r.ii’ 4’ (**1** §4), r.iii’. 9’ (**1** §5); **UM 29-15-617** o.ii’. 10 (**1** §1)

nam-tab “partnership”
- nam-tab-ba-še$_3$: **4** r.i. 12’, 25’, r.ii. 23’

niĝ$_2$ “thing, possession”
- niĝ$_2$ gub-ba: **4** r.ii. 28’
- še niĝ$_2$ u$_2$-gu ba-an-de$_2$: **CBS 8663+** r.i’. 1 (**3** §1); **MS 3176/5** r.i. 30 (**3** §1)

niĝ$_2$-ba “free gift, share”
- niĝ$_2$-ba-ni-še$_3$: **1** A.i. 8’; **CBS 8437** r. 10 (**1** §1); **MS 4979** o. 17 (-<<a-ni>>-) (**1** §1); **N 4075** o.ii’. 5’ (**1** §1)

niĝ$_2$-gur$_{11}$ “property”
- **4** r.iii. 8’

niĝ$_2$-ŠID “account, balance”
- **4** r.ii. 26’

si “to fill”
- bi-ib$_2$-si-si: **CBS 8663+** r.i’. 4 (**3** §1); **MS 3176/5** r.i. 33 (**3** §1); **UM 55-21-441** r.ii. 3’ (**3** §1)

si$_3$-ga “lot”
- si$_3$-ga-bi: **2** B.i. 2’; **4** o.iv. 6, r.i. 9’, 22’

si.g “to place”
- in-sig$_9$(-ge): **CBS 8663+** o.i. 5’ (**3** §1); **Ist Ni 1576** o.i. 2’ (**3** §1); **MS 3176/5** r.i. 20 (-ge) (**3** §1)
- sig$_9$-ge$_4$-de$_3$: **4** o.i. 3, 13, o.iii. 8**;** **6** o.i. 3; **N 1326** r.i. 9’ (**6** §1)

sig$_9$-ga “investment share”
- ud sig$_9$-ga-ne-ne-a: **4** r.ii. 25’
- **2** B.i. 5’; **4** r.ii. 20’, 22’

siki “wool”
- siki-ta-am$_3$ **9** o.i. 9’; **N 5863** r.ii’. 10’ (**1** §4)

siki-ba “wool ration”
- **N 5863** r.ii’. 11’ (**1** §4)

sila “street”
- sila$^?$-a ĝal$_2$-la-a-še$_3$: **6** o.i. 22

silim “(to be) healthy, in good condition”
- ^{ĝeš}ma$_2$ silim-ma: **1** C.i. 32, C.ii. 23; **3N-T567** o.i. 17 (**1** §11)

simug “smith, metalworker”
- **1** B.i. 9; **N 5863** r.iii’. 14’ (**1** §5)

su$_8$.g “to go” (plural)
- al-su$_8$-ge-ne$^?$: **CBS 2298** o. 11 (**2** §2)
- la-ba-an-su$_8$-ge-eš: **2** A.ii’. 1’; **CBS 2298** o. 14 (**2** §2)

sug$_6$ “to replace”
- in-na-su-su-e: **4** r.v. 3’
- mu še nu-mu-un-sug$_6$-ga-še$_3$: **MS 3176/5** o.iii’. 6 (**4** §6)
- mu še u$_3$ maš$_2$ nu-mu-un-sug$_6$-a-še$_3$: **4** o.iii. 12

ša$_{13}$-dub-ba-tuš-a “an official”
- **10** r.i’. 8’

šag$_4$ “heart; inside, in”
  cf. šag$_4$ ~ dug$_3$ “to satisfy”
- **3** A.i’. 2’; **4** r.iii. 19’; **CBS 8663+** o.i. 12’ (**3** §1); **Ist Ni 1576** o.i. 9’ (**3** §1)

- **4** r.ii. 24’, r.v. 11’

šu ~ šum$_2$ “to entrust, to hand over”
- šu ba-ab-šum$_2$: **4** r.ii. 29’

šu ~ tak$_4$ “to deliver”
- šu ba-ra-ab-tak$_4$: **4** r.iii. 10’

šu ~ te.ĝ “to receive”
- šu ba-an-ti: **2** A.ii’. 8’; **3** A.i’. 5’, A.ii’. 1’, B.ii’. 4’; **4** o.i. 6, o.ii. 11, o.iii. 1, 11, o.iv. 15, o.v. 6, r.i. 5’, 16’ r.iv. 15’, r.v. 8’; **5** o.i. 6, r.i’. 1, r.ii’. 19; **6** o.i. 6, 14, 25, 34; **7** o.i. 4; **11** 2’; **A 30173** o.i. 5 (**6** §3); **CBS 8663+** o.i. 15’ (**3** §1); **CBS 10288** o.ii’. 1’ (**6** §3); **CBS 10311** o.ii’. 1’ (**7**); **Ist Ni 10108** o.i. 4 (**7**); **MS 3176/5** o.iii’. 5 (**4** §6), 36 (**4** §9); **N 1326** r.ii. 2’ (**6** §3); **N 4567** o.i. 4 (**7**); **UM 29-13-408a** o.ii’. 7’ (**4** §9); **UM 29-16-482** o.ii’. 4 (**7**)
- šu ba-an-ti-eš: **CBS 2298** o. 8 (**2** §2)

šu-la$_2$ “a type of loan”
- **5** o.i. 2

šu-niĝin “total”
- **1** C.ii. 18

šum$_2$ “to give”
cf. šu ~ šum$_2$
- ba-ab-šum$_2$-mu-še$_3$: **MS 3176/5** o.iii’. 10 (**4** §6)
- ba-an-šum$_2$: **4** r.ii. 17’
- ba-(ra-)ab-šum$_2$-mu-ne: **2** A.ii’. 2’
- i$_3$-na-ab-šum$_2$-mu: **5** r.i’. 12
- in-na-an-šum$_2$: **CBS 1206** o.i’. 2’ (**1** §1); **MS 4979** o. 12 (**1** §1); **N 2469** o. 5’ (**1** §1)
- la-ba-an-šum$_2$: **4** o.ii. 16
- nu-mu-ni-in-šum$_2$: **4** r.i. 20’
- šum$_2$-mu-dam: **4** o.i. 8, o.ii. 13, o.iii. 3, r.i. 7’; **6** o.i. 8

tag “to touch”
- nu-mu-un-tag-ga: **MS 3176/5** o.iii’. 8 (**4** §6)

taḫ “to add”
- bi$_2$-ib-taḫ-e: **3** A.ii’. 10’; **5** r.i’. 24, r.ii’. 12; **6** o.i. 20
- taḫ-ḫe-dam: **4** o.iv. 12, o.v. 3; **5** r.ii’. 1, 16

tak$_4$ “to leave behind, to save, to keep back”
cf. kišib ~ tak$_4$
cf. šu ~ tak$_4$
- in-na-an-tak$_4$: **4** o.iii. 15; **MS 3176/5** o.iii’. 9 (**4** §6)

u$_2$-gu ~ de$_2$ "to disappear"

- u$_2$-gu ba-an-de$_2$: **1** C.iii. 20, D.i. 12; **4** o.ii. 3, o.v. 11; **CBS 8663+** r.i'. 1 (**3** §1); **MS 3176/5** o.iii'. 41 (**4** §9), r.i. 30 (**3** §1); **UM 29-13-408a** o.ii'. 12' (**4** §9)

u$_3$ "and"

- **1** A.i. 8', B.iii. 30, 35, C.i. 7, 11, 17, 33, C.ii. 24, C.iii. 21; **4** o.iii. 12, o.v. 7, r.i. 28'; **5** r.i'. 3; **6** o.i. 8; **9** o.i. 5'; **10** r.i'. 3'; **3N-T567** o.i. 18 (**1** §11); **CBS 2298** o. 7 (**2** §2); **CBS 8437** r. 10 (**1** §1); **CBS 8663+** o.i. 20' (**3** §1); **MS 3176/5** o.iii'. 37 (**4** §9), r.i. 29 (**3** §1); **MS 4979** o. 17 (**1** §1), r. 17 (**1** §9); **N 4075** o.ii'. 5' (**1** §1); **N 5863** r.ii'. 11' (**1** §4); **UM 29-13-408a** o.ii'. 8' (**4** §9); **UM 55-21-333** o.i. 2', 7' (**1** §9)

ud "day; when"

- ud buru$_{14}$-(a-)ka: cf. *s.v.* buru$_{14}$
- ud-da: **6** o.i. 15, 17
- ud 1-e: **5** o.i. 14
- ud til$_3$-la-ni-še$_3$: cf. *s.v.* til$_3$-la
- **4** r.ii. 25', r.iv. 21'; **5** o.i. 17, r.i'. 11, r.ii'. 5, 9, 20, 23; **MS 3176/5** o.iii'. 10 (**4** §6)

ud kur$_2$-še$_3$ "in future"

- **4** o.ii. 6, o.v. 14, r.iii. 28', r.iv. 7'; **9** o.i. 1'; **CBS 8437** r. 8 (**1** §1); **MS 3176/5** o.iv'. 1 (**4** §9); **MS 4979** o. 15 (**1** §1); **N 2469** o. 8' (**1** §1)

ug$_7$ "to die" (plural)

- ba-ug$_7$-a-ta: **1** C.i.9

uludin "due-time"

- ki uludin-bi-še$_3$: **6** o.i. 26, 29; **A 30173** o.i. 6, 9 (**6** §3); **CBS 10288** o.ii'. 2', 5' (**6** §3); **N 1326** r.ii. 3', 6' (**6** §3)

ur$_2$ "foundations"

- ur$_2$ e$_2$-a: **4** r.iii. 13'

ur$_3$ "roof"

- ur$_3$ e$_2$-a: **4** r.iii. 15'

ur$_3$ "to bake"

- šeg$_{12}$ al-ur$_3$-ra: **4** r.ii. 31'

us$_2$-sa-du "border"

- **4** r.iii. 20'

uš$_2$ "to die" (singular)

- ba-uš$_2$: **1** C.iii. 19
- ba-uš$_2$-a-ta: **1** A.i. 3', A.iii. x+9, B.ii. 27, B.iii. 12; **CBS 1206** o.i'. 7' (**1** §1); **CBS 8868** o.i. 9' (**1** §8); **IM 58639** o.ii'. 10' (**1** §8)

za$_3$-mi$_2$ "praise"

- ^{d}nisaba za$_3$-mi$_2$: **4** r.v. 14'

Akkadian word

5. Bibliography

BIBILIOGRAPHICAL ABBREVIATIONS

ABAW	Abhandlungen der Bayerischen Akademie der Wissenschaften
AfO	Archiv für Orientforschung
AHDO–RIDA	Archive d'Histoire du Droit Oriental–Revue Internationale des Droits de l'Antiquité
AOAT	Alter Orient und Altes Testament
ARES	Archivi Reali di Ebla, Studi
AS	Assyriological Studies
AuOr	Aula Orientalis
BBVO	Berliner Beiträge zum Vorderen Orient
BSA	Bulletin of Sumerian Agriculture
CAD	Chicago Assyrian Dictionary
CDLB	Cuneiform Digital Library Bulletin
CDLJ	Cuneiform Digital Library Journal
CDLN	Cuneiform Digital Library Notes
CM	Cuneiform Monographs
CUSAS	Cornell University Studies in Assyriology and Sumerology
DCCLT	Digital Corpus of Cuneiform Lexical Texts http://oracc.org/dcclt
FAOS	Freiburger altorientalische Studien
GMTR	Guides to the Mesopotamian Textual Record
HdO	Handbook of Oriental Studies. Section one, The Near and Middle East
JANER	Journal of Ancient Near Eastern Religions
JAOS	Journal of the American Oriental Society
JCS	Journal of Cuneiform Studies
JESHO	Journal of the Economic and Social History of the Orient
MARI	Mari Annales des Recherches Interdisciplinaires
MesCiv	Mesopotamian Civilizations
MHEM	Mesopotamian History and Environment Series, Memoirs
MSCT	Manuscripts in the Schøyen Collection: Cuneiform Texts
MSL	Materials for the Sumerian Lexicon
NABU	Nouvelles Assyriologiques Brèves et Utilitaires

OBMC	Old Babylonian Model Contracts http://oracc.org/obmc
OLZ	Orientalistische Literaturzeitung
OrAnt	Oriens Antiquus
OrNS	Orientalia Nova Series
RA	Revue d'Assyriologie
RGTC	Répertoire géographique des textes cunéiformes
RlA	Reallexikon der Assyriologie und Vorderasiatische Archäologie
SANER	Studies in Ancient Near Eastern Records
SANTAG	SANTAG Arbeiten und Untersuchungen zur Keilschriftkunde
SHCANE	Studies in the History and Culture of the Ancient Near East
SEL	Studi Epigrafici e Linguistici sul Vicino Oriente Antico
TMH	Texte und Materialien der Hilprecht-Collection
WAW	Writings from the Ancient World
ZA	Zeitschrift für Assyriologie und Vorderasiatische Archäologie
ZAR	Zeitschrift für Altorientalische und Biblische Rechtsgeschichte

BIBLIOGRAPHY

Al-Fouadi, A.H

1976 "Lexical Texts from Dhibā'ī", in B.L. Eichler, J.W. Heimerdinger, Å.W. Sjöberg (eds.), *Kramer Anniversary Volume. Cuneiform Studies in Honor of Samuel Noah Kramer*, *AOAT* 25, Neukirchen-Vluyn, 1–12.

Bodine, W.R.

2015 *How Mesopotamian Scribes Learned to Write Legal Documents. A Study of the Sumerian Model Contracts in the Babylonian Collection at Yale University*, Lewiston, NY.

Chambon, G. – M. Guichard

2015 "«Il faut que vos gardes soient fortes!». Une lettre de Sūmu-El sur la guerre entre Isin et Larsa", *Semitica* 57, 33–42.

Charpin, D.

1980 *Archives familiales et propriété privée en Babylonie ancienne: études des documents de Tell Sifr*, Hautes Études Orientales 12, Genève.

1986 *Le clergé d'Ur au siècle d'Hammurabi (XIXe–XVIIIe siècles av. J.-C.)*, Hautes Études Orientales 22, Genève.

1987 "Les Décrets Royaux à l'Époque Paléo-Babylonienne, à Propos d'une Ouvrage Récente", *AfO* 34, 36–44.

1990 "L'*andurârum* à Mari", *MARI* 6, 253–270.

2008 "Compte rendu: J. Hengstl, U. Sick. (eds.), *Recht gestern und heute. Festschrift zum 85. Geburtstag von Richard Haase*, Philippika 13, Wiesbaden, 2006", *RA* 102, 187–188.

2009 "En marge d'ARCHIBAB, 1: *šipirtum* «gage» en paléo-babylonien", *NABU* 2009/59.

2015 "Chroniques bibliographiques 17. Six nouveaux recueils de documents paléo-babyloniens", *RA* 109, 143–196.

2017 "Chroniques bibliographiques 20. Pour une diplomatique des documents paléo-babyloniens", *RA* 111, 155–178.

Civil, M.

1969 "Old Babylonian Proto-Lu", in E. Reiner and M. Civil (eds.), *The Series lu_2 = ša and Related Texts*, *MSL* 12, Roma, 24–73.

1974–1977 "Enlil and Namzitarra", *AfO* 25, 65–71.

1979 *Ea A = nâqu, Aa A = nâqu, with their Forerunners and Related Texts*, *MSL* 14, Roma.

1994 *The Farmer's Instructions. A Sumerian Agricultural Manual. AuOr Supplementa* 5, Barcelona.

2006 "The Song of the Millstone" in G. del Olmo Lete, L. Feliu, A. Millet Albà (eds.), *Šapal tibnim mû illakū. Studies Presented to Joaquín Sanmartín on the Occasion of his 65th Birthday, AuOr Supplementa* 22, Barcelona, 121–138.

2008 *The Early Dynastic Practical Vocabulary A (Archaic HAR-ra A)*, *ARES* 4, Roma.

2011 "The Law Collection of Ur-Namma", in A.R. George (ed.), *Cuneiform Royal Inscriptions and Related Texts in the Schøyen Collection*, *CUSAS* 17, Bethesda, 221–286.

Claassens-van Wyk, S.J.

2013 "Old Babylonian Nippur solutions between beneficiaries in a deceased estate division agreement", *Journal for Semitics* 22/1, 56–89.

Cohen, M. E.

1993 *The Cultic Calendars of the Ancient Near East*, Bethesda.

Crisostomo, C.J.

2015 "Writing Sumerian, Creating Texts: Reflections on Text-building Practices in Old Babylonian Schools", *JANER* 15, 121–142.

forthcoming *Translation as Scholarship: Language, Writing, and Bilingual Education in Ancient Babylonia. SANER. De Gruyter*

David, M.

1927 *Die Adoption im altbabylonischen Recht*, Leipzig.

Delnero, P.

2013 "On the Sumerian Liturgical Tradition", *OLZ* 108: 145–151.

Dole, G.F.

1965 *Partnership Loans in the Old Babylonian Period*, PhD Dissertation, Harvard University.

Dombradi, E.

1996 *Die Darstellung des Rechtsaustrags in den altbabylonischen Prozessurkunden*, *FAOS* 20, Stuttgart.

Driver, G.R. – J.C. Miles

1955 *The Babylonian Laws*, Oxford.

Durand, J.-M.

1990 "Documents pour l'histoire du royaume de Haute-Mesopotamie II", *MARI* 6, 271–301.

Edzard, D.O.

1975 "Zum sumerischen Eid", in S.J. Lieberman (ed.) *Sumerological Studies in Honor of Thorkild Jacobsen on His Seventieth Birthday, June 7, 1974*, *AS* 20, Chicago, 63–98.

1976–1980 "IM", *RlA* 5, 63–65.

Eilers, W.

1931 *Gesellschaftsformen im altbabylonischen Recht*, Leipziger rechtswissenschaftliche Studien, Heft 65, Leipzig.

Ellis, M.d.J.

1975 "An Old Babylonian adoption contract from Tell Harmal", *JCS* 27, 130–151.

Englund, R.K.

1988 "Administrative timekeeping in ancient Mesopotamia", *JESHO* 31, 121–185.

1990 *Organisation und Verwaltung der Ur III-Fischerei*, *BBVO* 10, Berlin.

2010 "BU!", in A. Kleinerman, J.M. Sasson (eds.), *Why Should Someone Who Knows Something Conceal It? Cuneiform Studies in Honor of David I. Owen on His 70th Birthday*, Bethesda, 95–114.

2011 "The State of CDLI's Ur III Transliterations", *CDLN* 2011: 4.

Falkenstein, A.

1956 *Die neusumerischen Gerichtsurkunden, Erster Teil. Einleitung und systematische Darstellung*, *ABAW*, N.F. 39, München.

Farber, G.

2005 "SAG as Pars Pro Toto for 'Person' and 'Dead Body.'", in Y. Sefati *et al.* (eds.), *"An Experienced Scribe Who Neglects Nothing": Ancient Near Eastern Studies in Honor of Jacob Klein*, Bethesda, 108–115.

Fitzgerald, M.A.

2003 "pisan-dub-ba and the Direction of Cuneiform Script", *CDLB* 2003: 2.

Friberg, J.

2007 *A Remarkable Collection of Babylonian Mathematical Texts*, *MSCT* 1, New York.

Gelb, I.J.

1982 Terms for Slaves in Ancient Mesopotamia", in M.A. Dandamayev *et al.* (eds.), *Societies and Languages of the Ancient Near East, Studies in Honour of I.M. Diakonoff*, Warminster, 81–98.

George, A.R.

2009 *Babylonian Literary Texts in the Schøyen Collection*, *CUSAS* 10, Bethesda.

Gibson, McG. – D.P. Hansen – R.L. Zettler

1998–2001 "Nippur B. Archäologisch", *RlA* 9, 546–565.

Goddeeris, A.

2009 *Tablets from Kisurra in the Collections of the British Museum*, *SANTAG* 9, Wiesbaden.

2016 *The Old Babylonian Legal and Administrative Texts in the Hilprecht Collection Jena*, *TMH* 10, Wiesbaden.

Groneberg, B.

1980 *Die Orts- und Gewässernamen der altbabylonischen Zeit*, *RGTC* 3, Wiesbaden.

Hallo, W.W.

1975 "Toward a History of Sumerian Literature", in S.J. Lieberman (ed.) *Sumerological Studies in Honor of Thorkild Jacobsen on His Seventieth Birthday, June 7, 1974*, *AS* 20, Chicago, 181–203.

Harris, R.
1963 "The organisation and administration of the cloister in ancient Babylonia", *JESHO* 6/2, 121–157.
1975 *Ancient Sippar: A Demographic Study of an Old Babylonian City (1894-1595 B.C.)*, Leiden.

Kienast, B.
1978 *Die altbabylonischen Briefe und Urkunden aus Kisurra, FAOS* 2/1, Wiesbaden.

Klein, J. – T.M. Scharlach
2007 "A Collection of Model Court Cases from Old Babylonian Nippur (CBS 11324)", *ZA* 97, 1–25.

Kleinerman, A.
2011 *Education in Early 2nd Millennium Babylonia. The Sumerian Epistolary Miscellany*, *CM* 42, Leiden–Boston.

Koschaker, P.
1931 *Über einige griechische Rechtsurkunden aus den östlichen Randgebieten des Hellenismus: mit Beiträgen zum Eigentums- und Pfandbegriff nach griechischen und orientalischen Rechten*, Leipzig.

Kraus, F.R.
1951 "Nippur und Isin nach altbabylonischen Rechtsurkunden", *JCS* 3, 1–228.

Lautner, J.G.
1939 "Altbabylonische Gesellschaftsverhältnisse – Studien zum Miteigentum im altbabylonischen Recht II", in *Festschrift für Paul Koschaker*, Bd. III, Weimar, 24–79.

Limet, H.
2000 "Documents sumériens des Musées Royaux d'Art et d'Histoire", Akkadica 117, 1–20.

Malul, M.
1988 *Studies in Mesopotamian Legal Symbolism*, *AOAT* 221, Neukirchen–Vluyn.

Mendelsohn, I.
1949 *Slavery in the Ancient Comparative Study of Slavery in Babylonia, Assyria, Syria, and Palestine, from the Middle of the Third Millennium to the End of the First Millennium,* New York.

Meyer-Laurin, V.
2010 "Die *marû*-Basen der sumerischen Verben tum 'hin-, wegführen' und ře/de$_6$ 'bringen, liefern'", *ZA* 100, 1–14.

Michalowski, P.
1977 "Ur III Topographical Names", *OrAnt* 16, 287–296.

Muffs, Y.
1968 *Studies in the Aramaic Legal Papyri from Elephantine*, Leiden.

Neumann, H.

2004 "Prozeßführung im Edubba'a. Zu einigen Aspekten der Aneignung juristischer Kenntnisse im Rahmen des Curriculums babylonischer Schreiberausbildung", *ZAR* 10, 71–92.

Peterson, J.

2009 *Godlist from Old Babylonian Nippur in the University Museum, Philadelphia*, *AOAT* 362, Münster.

Pientka-Hinz, R.

2006 "Der *rabi sikkatum* in altbabylonischer Zeit", in J. Hengstl and U. Sick (eds.), *Recht gestern und heute. Festschrift zum 85. Geburtstag von Richard Haase*, Philippika 13, Wiesbaden, 53–70.

Powell, M.

1982 "Metrological Notes on the Esagila Tablet and Related Matters", *ZA* 72, 106–123.

1992 "Timber production in presargonic Lagaš", *BSA* 6, 99–122.

Prang, E.

1976 "Das Archiv des Imgua", *ZA* 66, 1–44.

Proust, C.

2007 *Tablettes mathématiques de Nippur*, Paris.

2008 *Tablettes mathématiques de la collection Hilprecht. Avec la collaboration de Manfred Krebernik et Joachim Oelsner. TMH* 8, Wiesbaden.

2012 "Reading colophons from Mesopotamian clay tablets dealing with mathematics", *NTM Zeitschrift für Geschichte der Wissenschaften, Technik und Medizin*, 20, 123–156.

Radner, K.

2001 "The Neo-Assyrian period", in R. Westbrook and R. Jasnow (eds.), *Security for Debt in Ancient Near Eastern Law*, Leiden–Boston–Köln, 265–288.

Robertson, J.F.

1984 "The Internal Political and Economic Structure of Old Babylonian Nippur: the *Guennakkum* and his 'house'", *JCS 36*, 145–190.

Roth, M.T.

1979 *Scholastic Tradition and Mesopotamian Law: a Study of FLP 1287, a Prism in the Collection of the Free Library of Philadelphia. PhD* Dissertation, University of Pennsylvania, UMI Ann Arbor.

1995 *Law Collections from Mesopotamia and Asia Minor*, *WAW* 6, Atlanta.

Sallaberger, W.

1996 *Der babylonische Töpfer und seine Gefässe nach Urkunden altsumerischer bis altbabylonischer Zeit sowie lexikalischen und literarischen Zeugnissen*, MHEM 3, Ghent.

2005 "'bringen' im Sumerischen. Lesung und Bedeutung von de_6(DU) und túm(DU)", in R. Rollinger (ed.), *Von Sumer bis Homer. Festschrift für Manfred Schretter zum 60. Geburtstag am 25. Februar 2004, AOAT* 325, Münster, 557–576.

2008 "Der Eid im Gerichtsverfahren in neusumerischen Umma", in P. Michalowski (ed.), *On the Third Dynasty of Ur: Studies in Honor of Marcel Sigrist, JCS Supplementary Series* 1, Boston, 159–176.

Schorr, M.

1913 *Urkunden des altbabylonischen Zivil- und Prozessrechts*, Leipzig.

Sigrist, M.

1992 *Drehem*, Bethesda.

Skaist, A.

1994 *The Old Babylonian Loan Contract. Its History and Geography*, Ramat Gan.

Spada, G.

2011 "A Handbook from the Eduba'a: An Old Babylonian Collection of Model Contracts", *ZA* 101, 204–245.

2012 "I modelli di contratto nell'edubba paleo-babilonese. Un esempio di contratto di adozione", *Annali dell'Università degli Studi di Napoli "L'Orientale"* 72, 133–148.

2014 "Two Old Babylonian Model Contracts", *CDLJ* 2014: 2.

2017a "The Sumerian verb kušur, 'to repair'", *NABU* 2017/4, 162–163.

2017b "Review of Walter Ray Bodine: How Mesopotamian Scribes Learned to Write Legal Documents. A Study of the Sumerian Model Contracts in the Babylonian Collection at Yale University", *ZA* 107, 290–306.

forthcoming "I *model contracts* nella tradizione scribale dell'Edubba paleo-babilonese", in G. Spada (ed.), *Ordinare il mondo*, Roma.

Sperl, G.

1967 "Diskussionsbeitrag zur Herstellung der 'Mikrotontafeln'", *OrNS* 36, 339–344.

Steinert, U.

2012 *Aspekte des Menschseins im Alten Mesopotamien. Eine Studie zu Person und Identität im 2. und 1. Jt. v. Chr., CM* 44, Leiden–Boston.

Steinkeller, P.

1981 "The Renting of Fields in Early Mesopotamia and the Development of the Concept of 'Interest' in Sumerian", *JESHO* 24/2, 113–145.

1989 *Sale documents of the Ur III period. FAOS* 17, Stuttgart.

2002 "Money-Lending Practices in Ur III Babylonia: The Issue of Economic Motivation", in M. Hudson and M. Van De Mieroop (eds.), *Debt and Economic Renewal in the Ancient Near East*, Bethesda, 109–137.

Stol, M.

1991 "Old Babylonian Personal Names", *SEL* 8, 191–212.

1993–1995 "Miete B.I. Altbabylonisch", *RlA* 8/3-4, 162–174.

1998 "Care of the Elderly in Mesopotamia in the Old Babylonian Period", in M. Stol and S.P. Vleeming (eds.), *The Care of the Elderly in the Ancient Near East*, *SHCANE* 14, Leiden–Boston–Köln, 59–118.

2009 "'To be ill' in Akkadian: the verb *salā'u* and the substantive *sili'tu*", in A. Attia and G. Buisson (eds.), *Advances in Mesopotamian Medicine from Hammurabi to Hippocrates. Proceedings of the International Conference "Oeil malade et mauvais oeil", Collège de France, Paris, 23rd June 2006*, *CM* 37, Leiden–Boston, 29–46.

2010 "Review of M.T. Roth (Hg.), *The Assyrian Dictionary of the Oriental Institute of the University of Chicago T and Ṭ*", *OLZ* 105, 170–179.

2011 "Sklave. Sklaverei. B. Altbabilonisch", *RlA* 12, 561–574.

2017 "Ziegel. A. Philologisch", *RlA* 15, 272–279.

Stone, E.C.

1982 "The Social Role of the *nadītu* Women in Old Babylonian Nippur", *JESHO* 25, 50–70.

Stone, E.C. – D.I Owen

1991 *Adoption in Old Babylonian Nippur and the Archive of Mannum-Mešu-Liṣṣur*, *MesCiv* 3, Winona Lake.

Studevent-Hickman, B.

2007 "The Ninety-Degree Rotation of the Cuneiform Script", in J. Cheng and M.H. Feldman (eds.), *Ancient Near Eastern Art in Context. Studies in Honor of Irene J. Winter by Her Students*. Leiden–Boston, 485–513.

Szlechter, E.

1947 *Le Contrat de société en Babylone, en Grèce, et à Rome: Etude de droit comparé de l'antiquité*, Paris.

1952 "L'affranchissement en droit suméro-akkadien", *AHDO–RIDA* 1, 125–195.

Tinney, S.

1999 "On the Curricular Setting of Sumerian Literature." *Iraq* 61, 159–172.

Van de Mieroop, M.

1992 "Wood in the Old Babylonian texts from Ur", *BSA* 6, 155–161.

Vandorpe, L.

2010 *Thy name is slave? The slave onomasticon of Old Babylonian Sippar*. Diss. Master, Ghent University.

Veenhof, K.R.

1982 "A deed of manumission and adoption from the late Old Assyrian period", in G. Van Driel, Th.J.H. Krispijn, M. Stol and K.R. Veenhof (eds.), *Zikir Sumin. Assyriological Studies Presented to F.R. Kraus on the Occasion of his Seventieth Birthday*, Leiden, 359–385.

2004 "Pfand", *RlA* 10, 439–449.

Veldhuis, N.

1997 *Elementary Education at Nippur. The Lists of Trees and Wooden Objects.* Unpublished doctoral thesis, University of Groningen.

2014 *History of the Cuneiform Lexical Tradition*, *GMTR* 6, Münster.

Vosmer, T.

2008 "Shipping in the Bronze Age: How Large was a 60-gur Ship?", in E. Olijdam and R.H. Spoor (eds.), *Intercultural relations between South and Southwest Asia. Studies in commemoration of E.C.L. During Caspers (1934-1996)*, BAR International Series 1826, Oxford, 230–235.

Westbrook, R.

1991 "The Phrase 'His Heart Is Satisfied' in Ancient Near Eastern Legal Sources", *JAOS* 111, 219–224.

1995 "Slave and Master in Ancient Near Eastern Law", *Chicago-Kent Law Review* 70, 1631–1676.

2001 "The Old Babylonian period", in R. Westbrook and R. Jasnow (eds.), *Security for Debt in Ancient Near Eastern Law*, Leiden–Boston–Köln, 63–92.

2003 "Old Babylonian period", in R. Westbrook (ed.), *A History of Ancient Near Eastern Law*, *HdO* 72, Leiden–Boston, 361–430.

Widell, M.

2002 "A Note on the Expression SI-ge$_4$-de$_3$/dam", *Sefarad* 62, 393–400.

Wilson, M.

2008 *Education in the Earliest Schools. Cuneiform Manuscripts in the Cotsen Collection*, Los Angeles.

Yoda, I.

1993 *Oaths in Sumerian Archival Texts: A Case Study of Ur III Nippur*, unpublished PhD dissertation, Yale University.

Zólyomi, G.

2017 *An Introduction to the Grammar of Sumerian*, Budapest.

Plates

All handcopies and photographs of cuneiform tablets are by Gabriella Spada.
In order to present the reader with the most legible views, they are reproduced here on a scale of 120% (nos. 2, 3, 5, 7, 10 and 11), except for nos. 1, 6 and 9 which are in full-scale, and no. 4, the micro-tablet, on a scale of 250%.

1 Side A

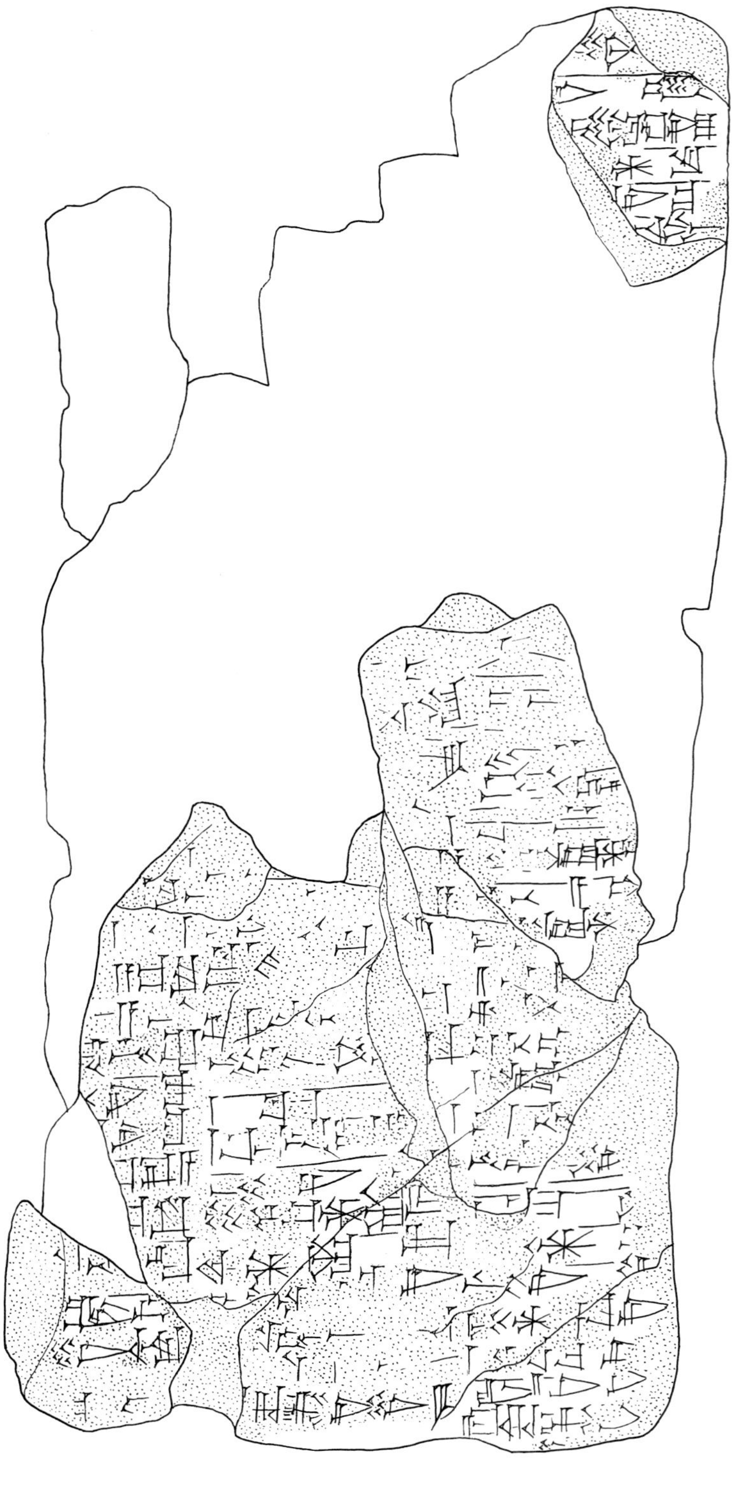

1 Side B

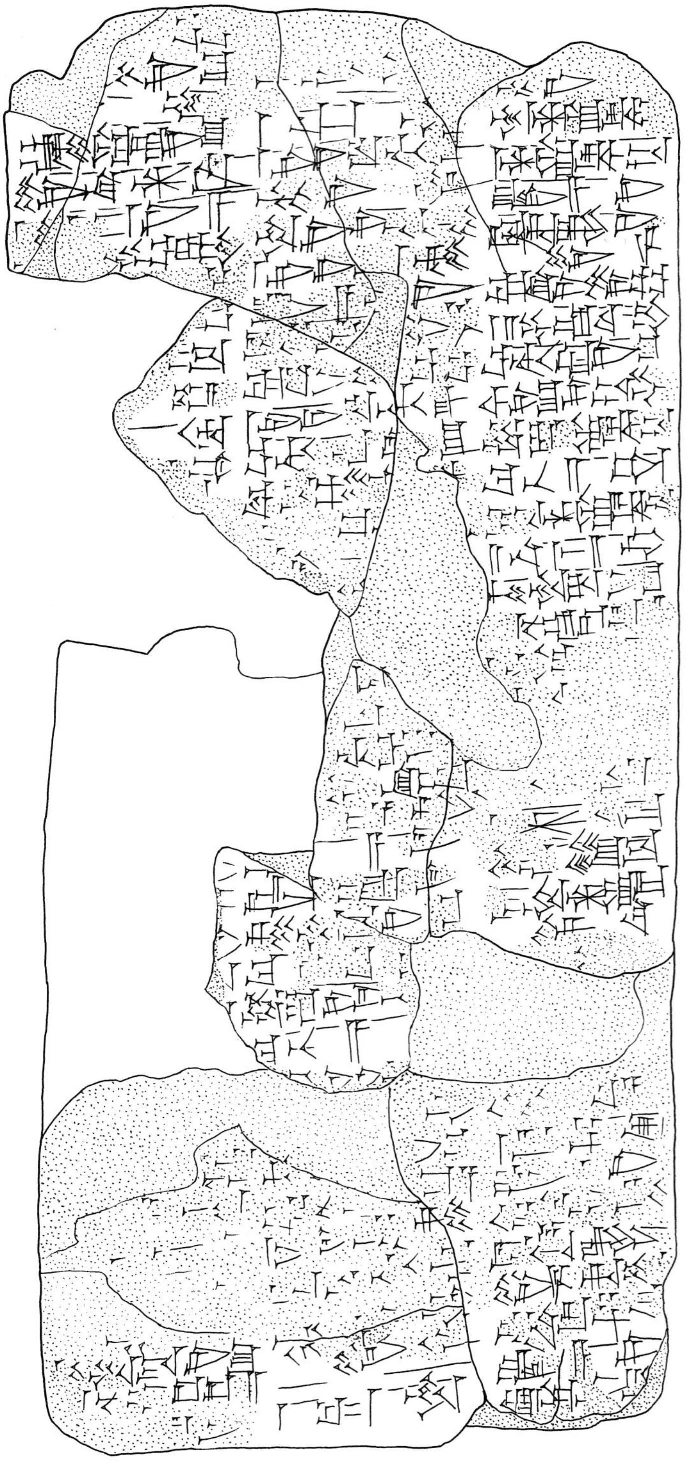

1 Side C

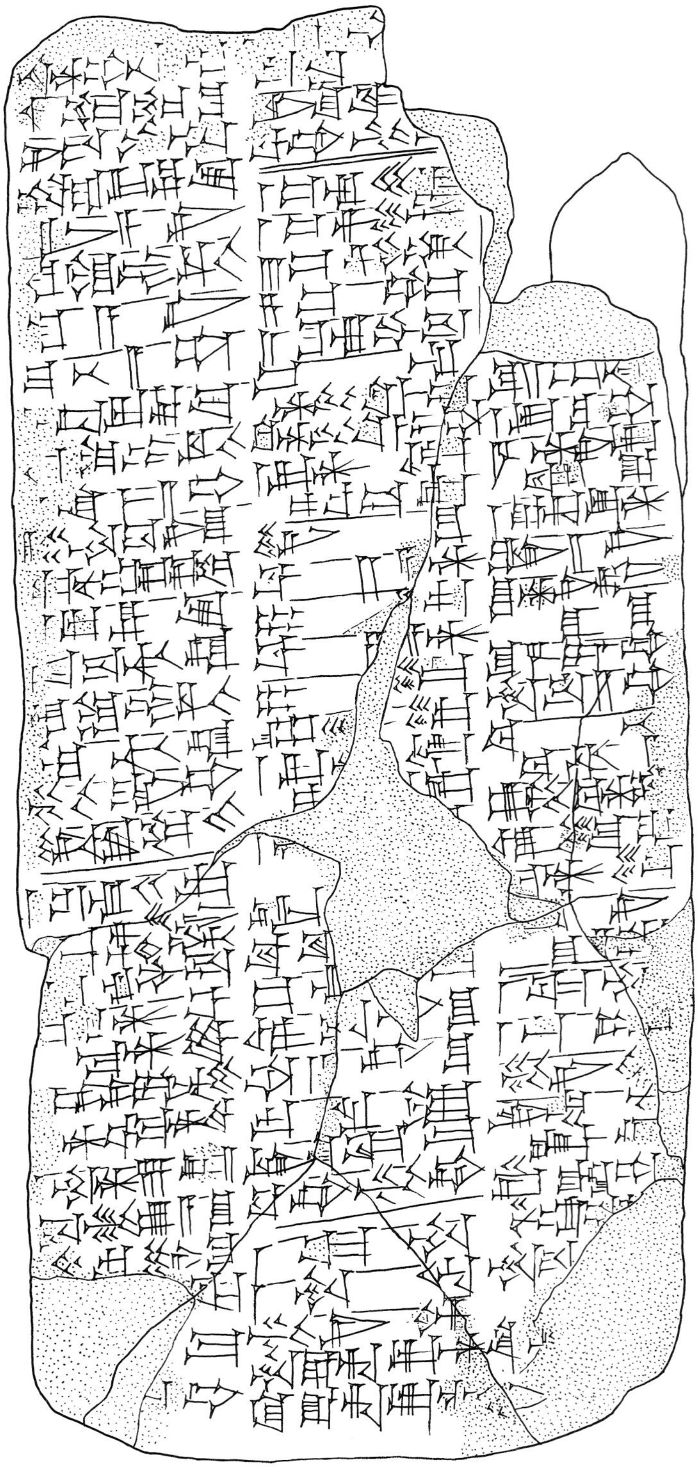

1 Side D

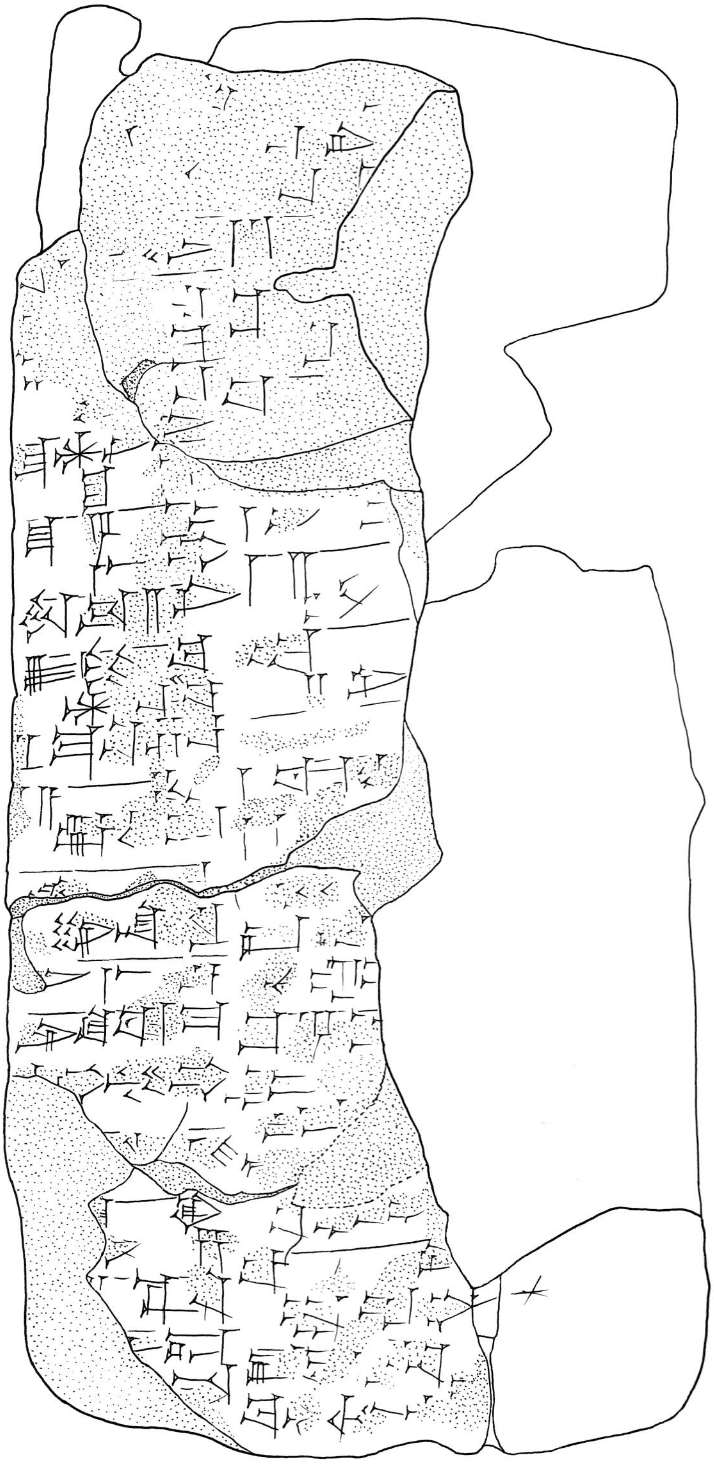

2

Side A

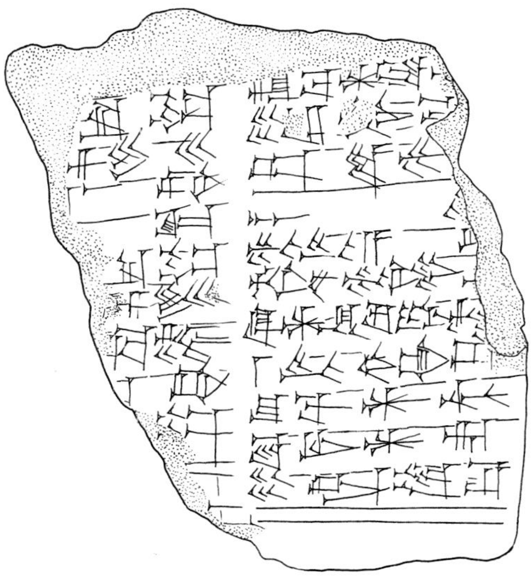

Side B

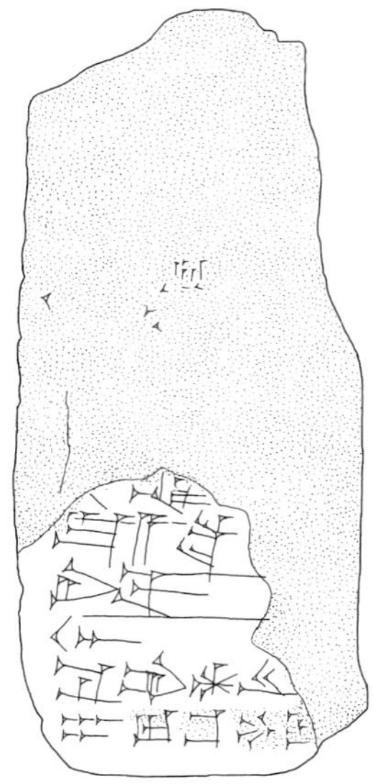

3

Side A

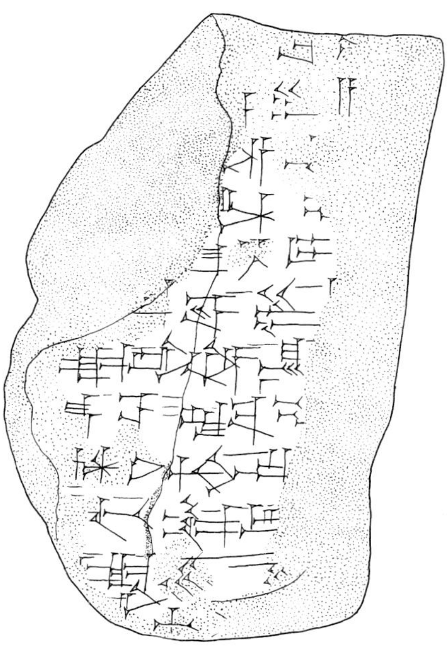

Side B

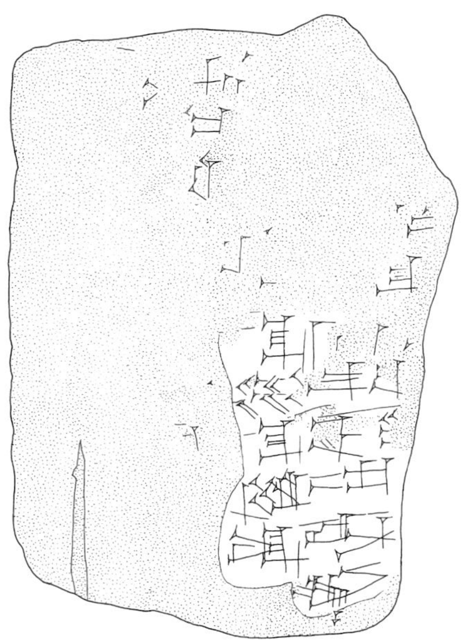

Text 4 – Obverse

Obv.

4

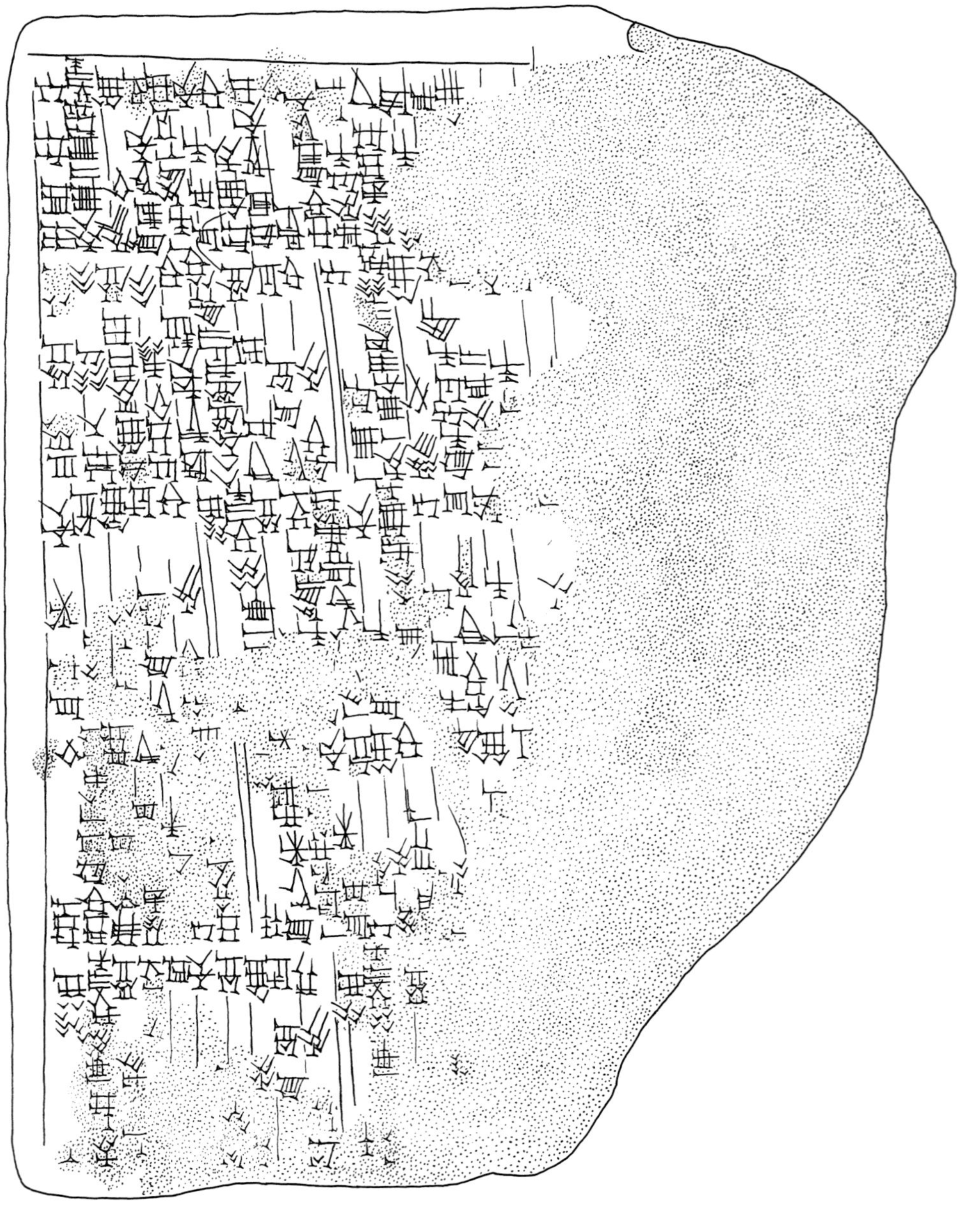

Rev. 4

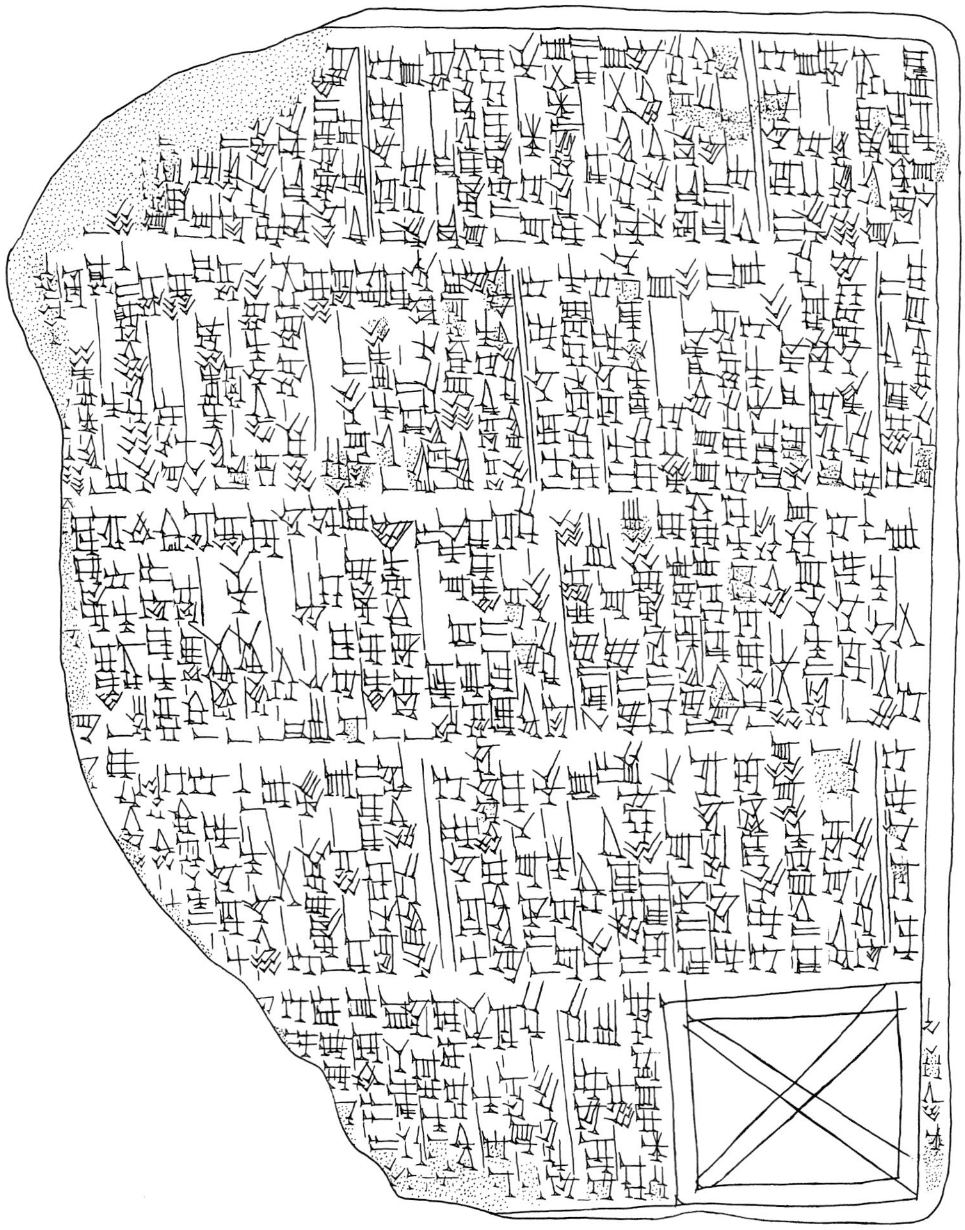

5

Obv.

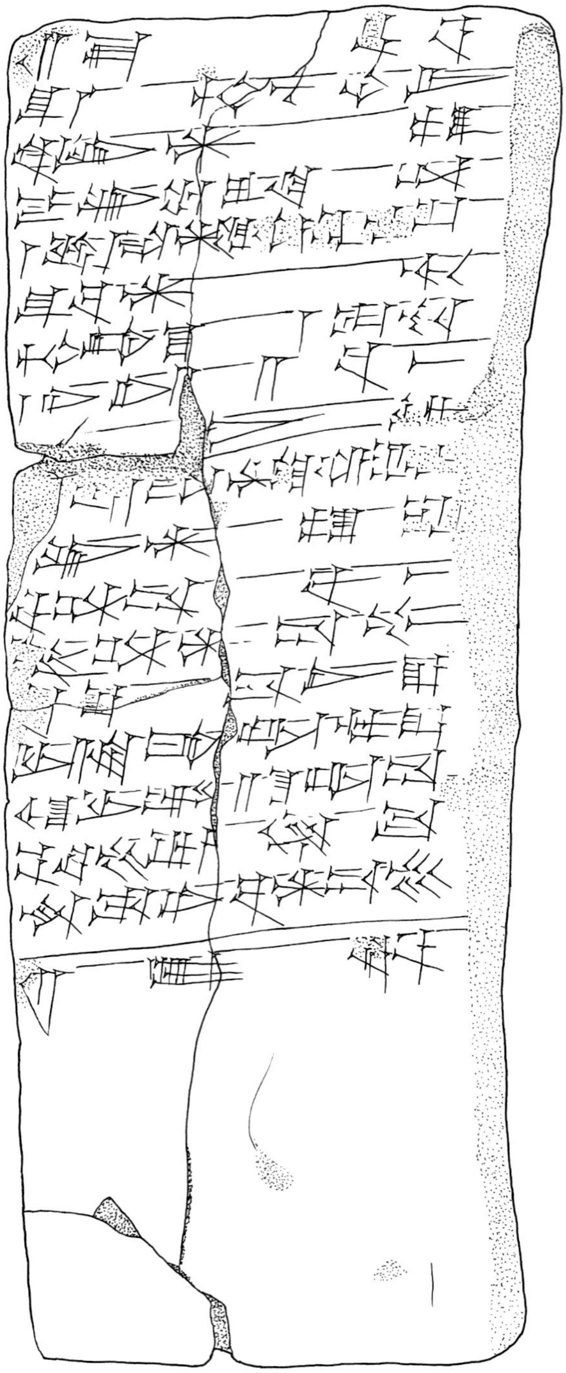

5

Rev.

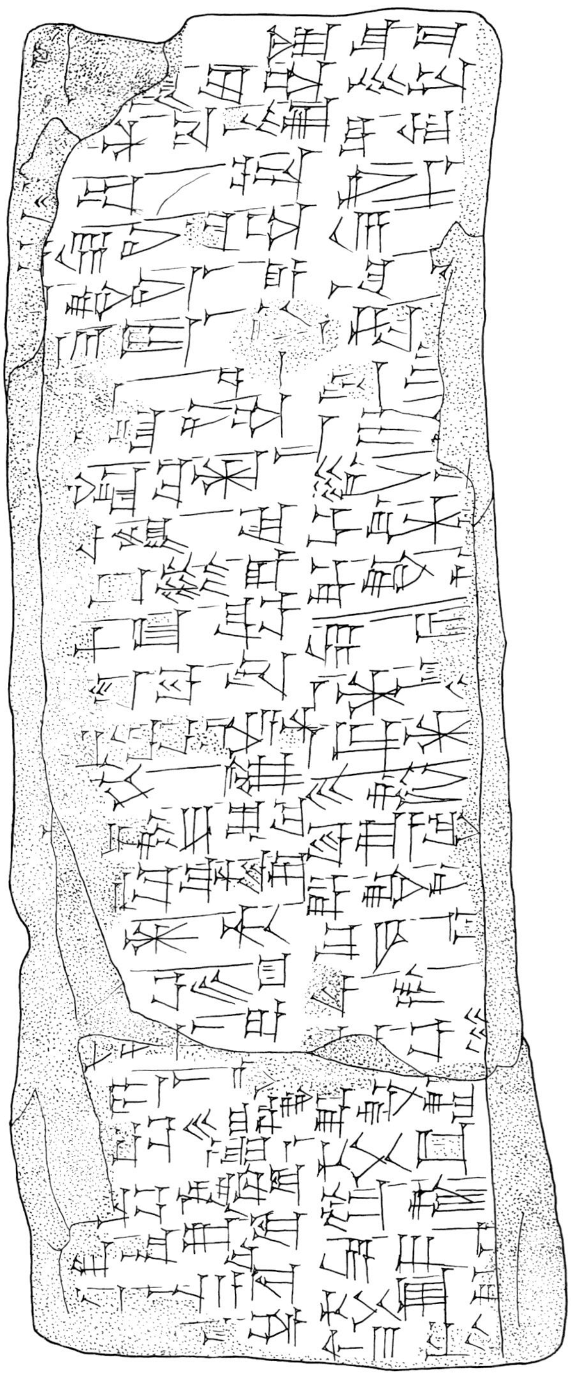

6

Obv.

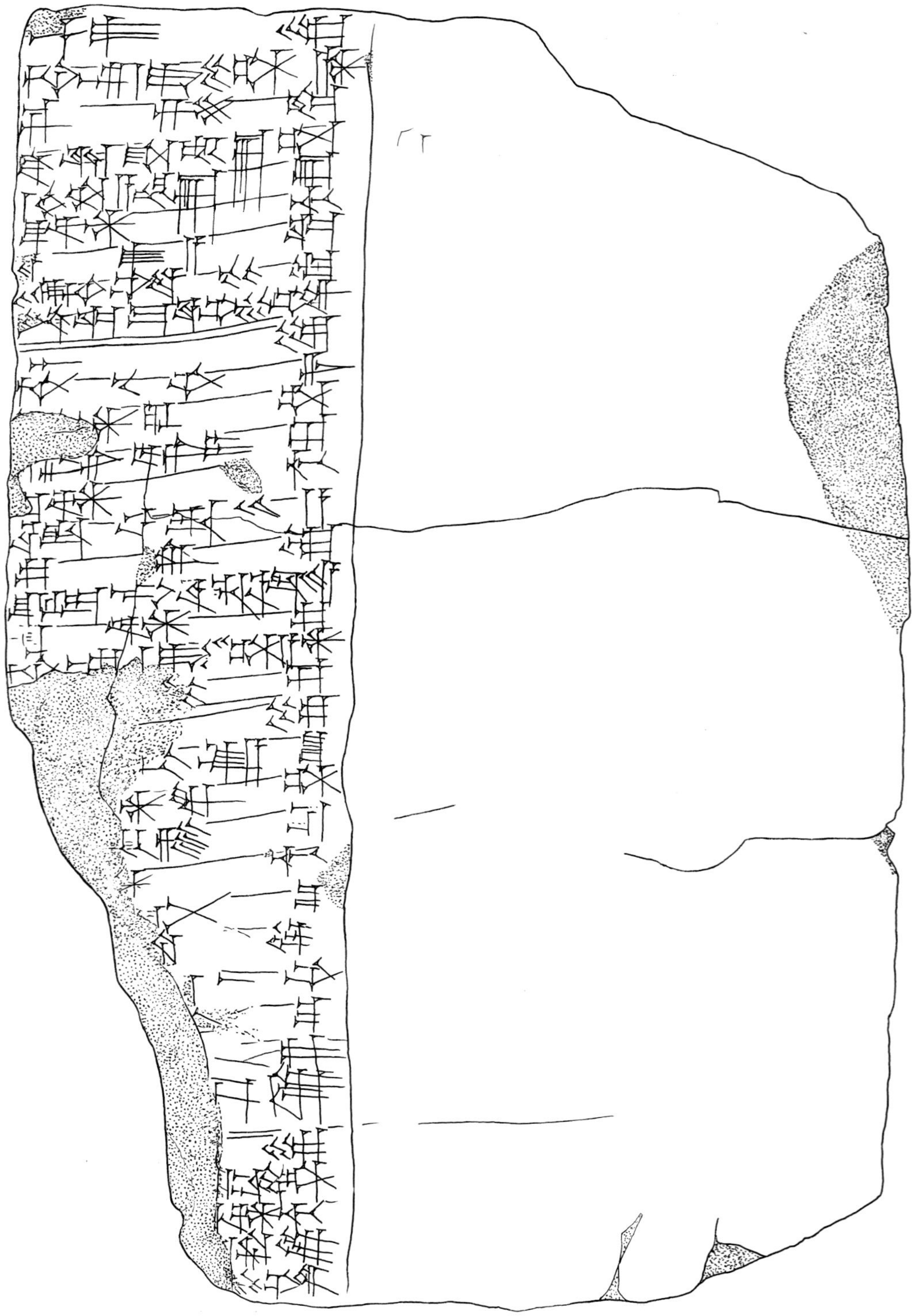

6

Rev.

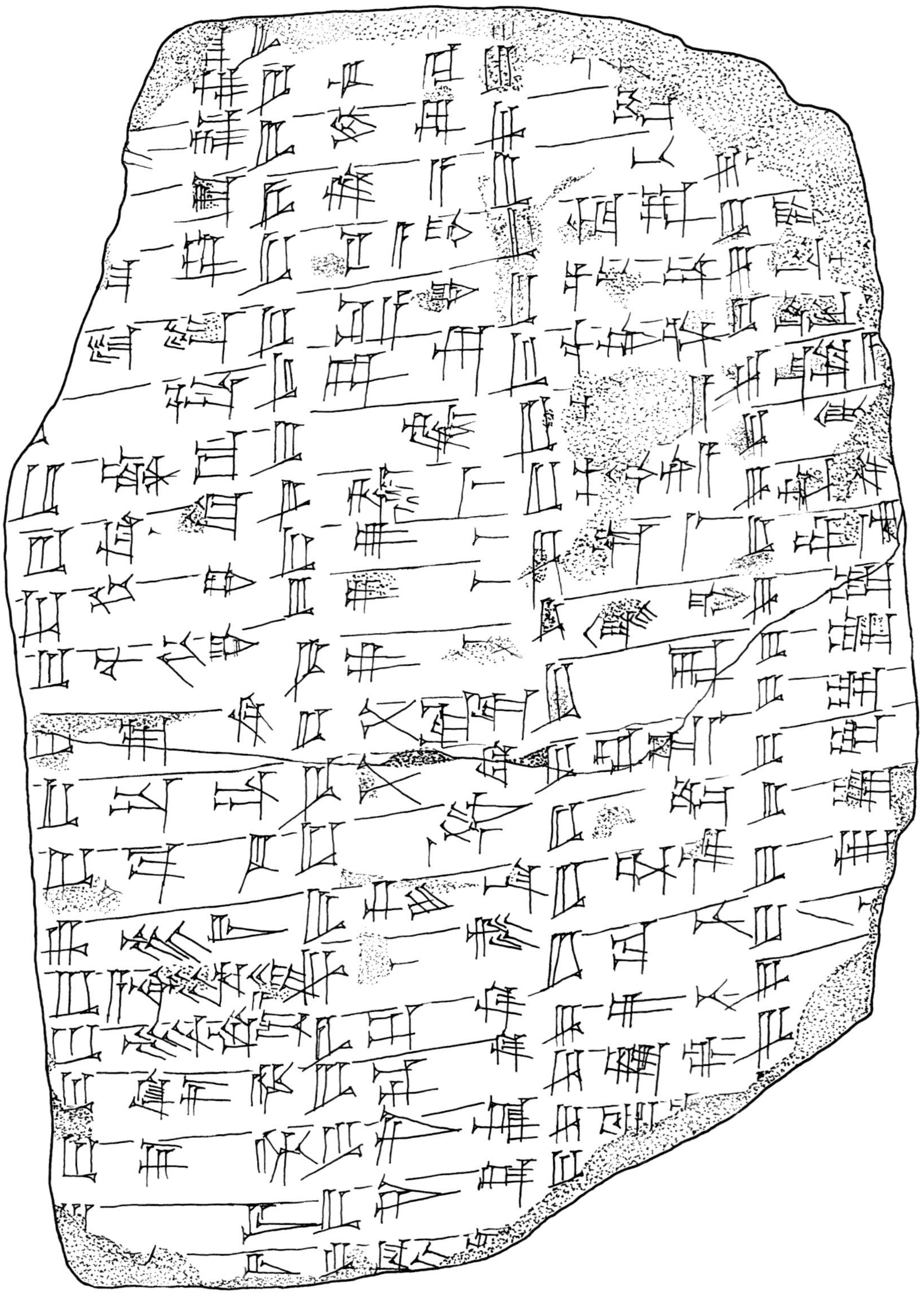

7

Obv.

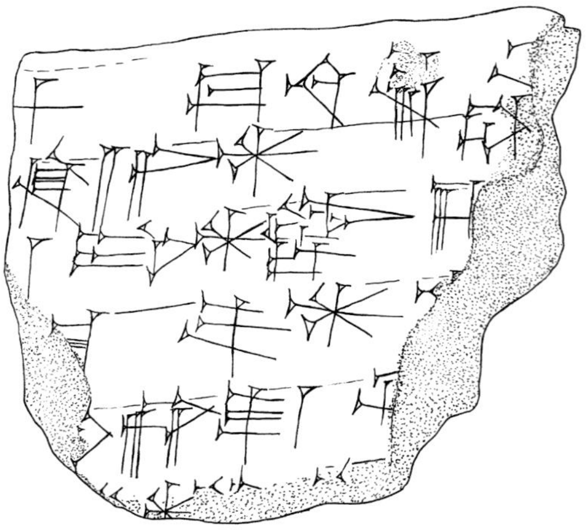

Rev.

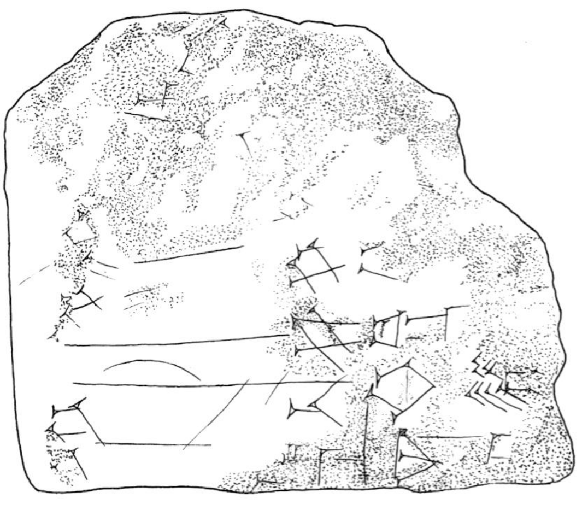

8

Obv.

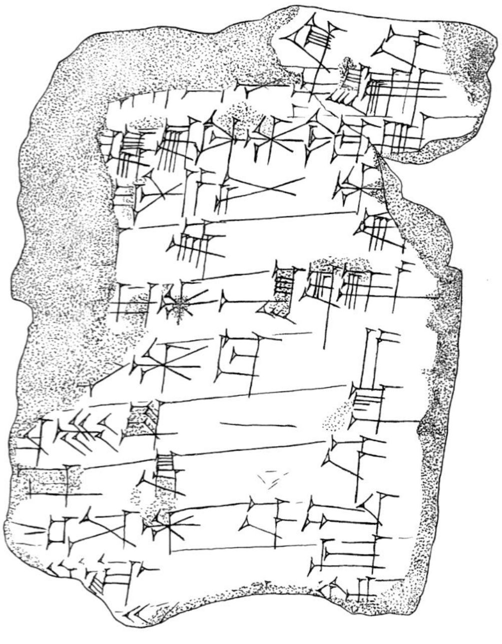

Rev.

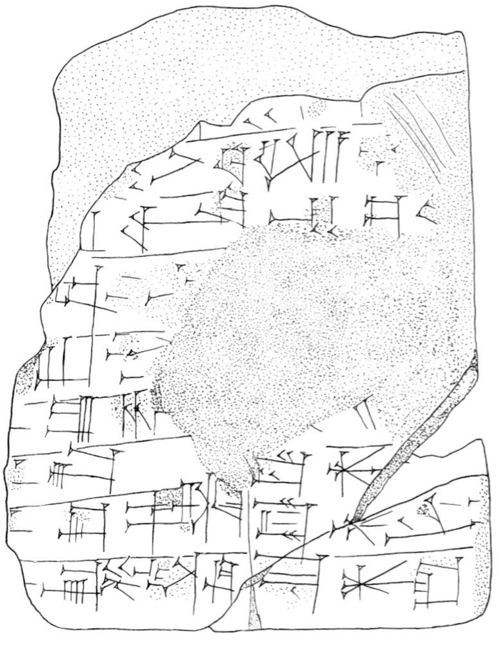

9

Obv.

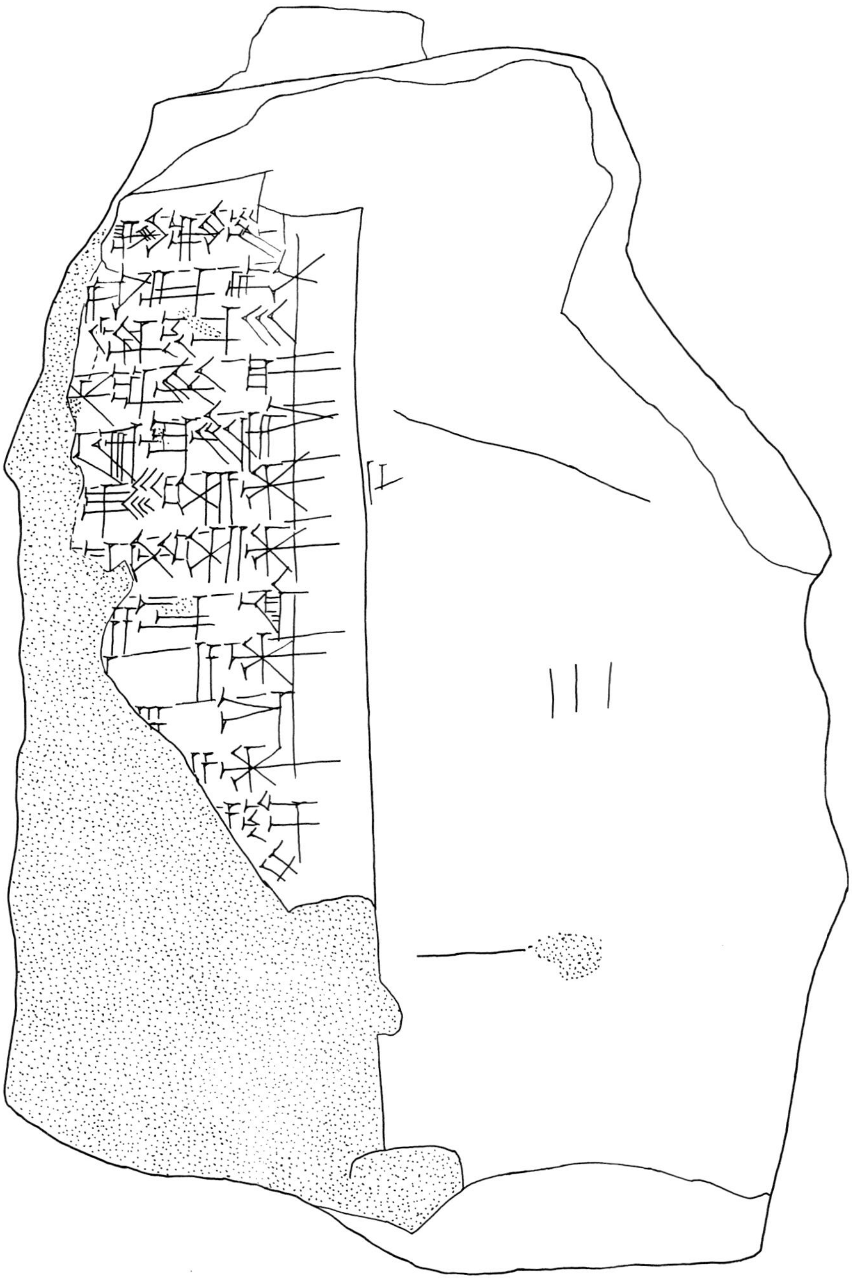

9

Rev.

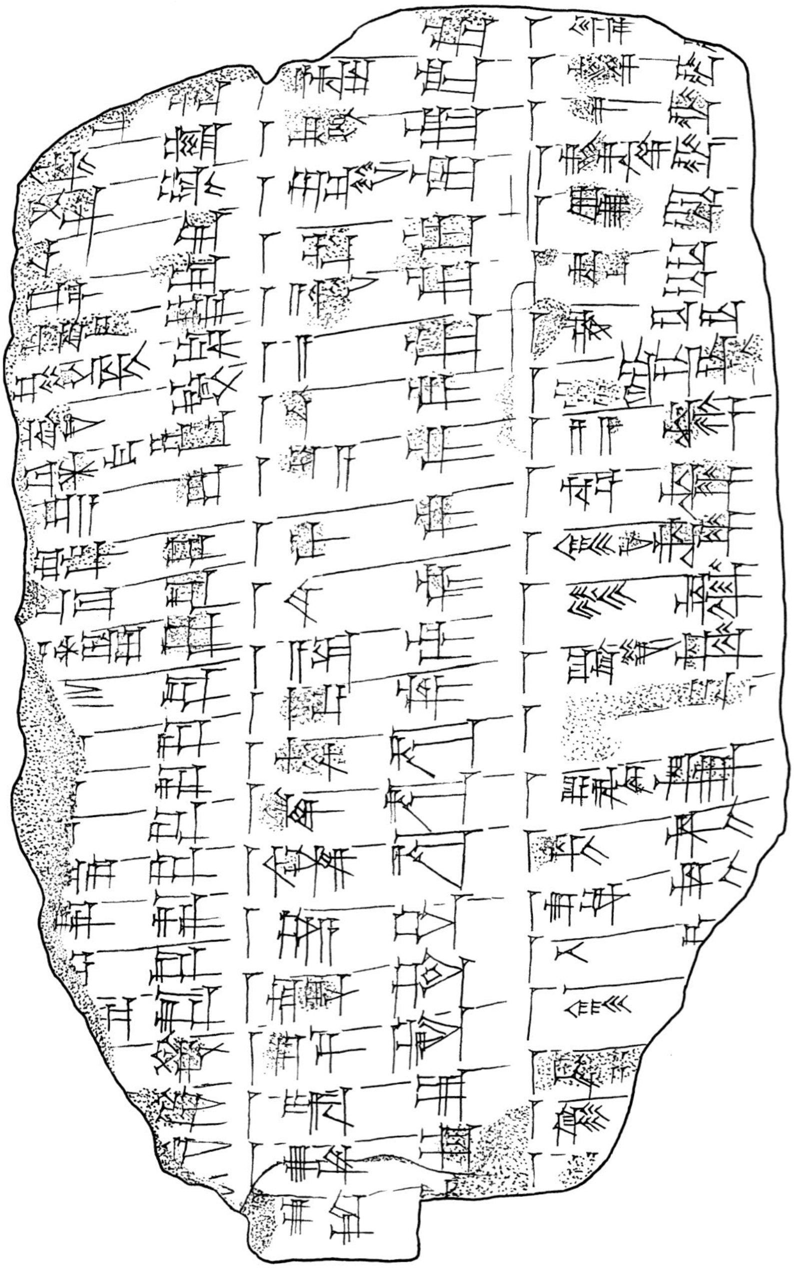

Obv.

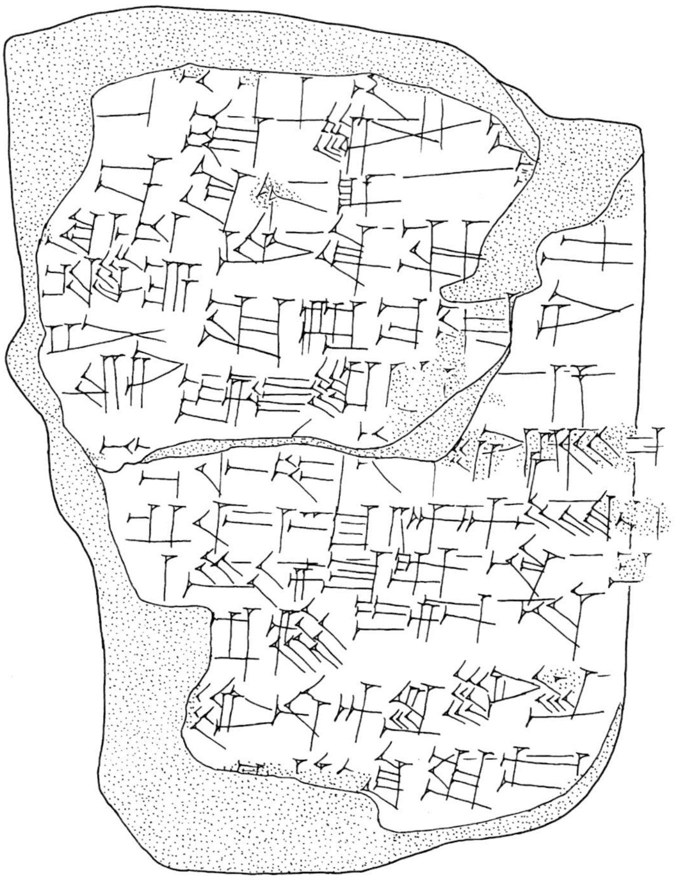

10

Rev.

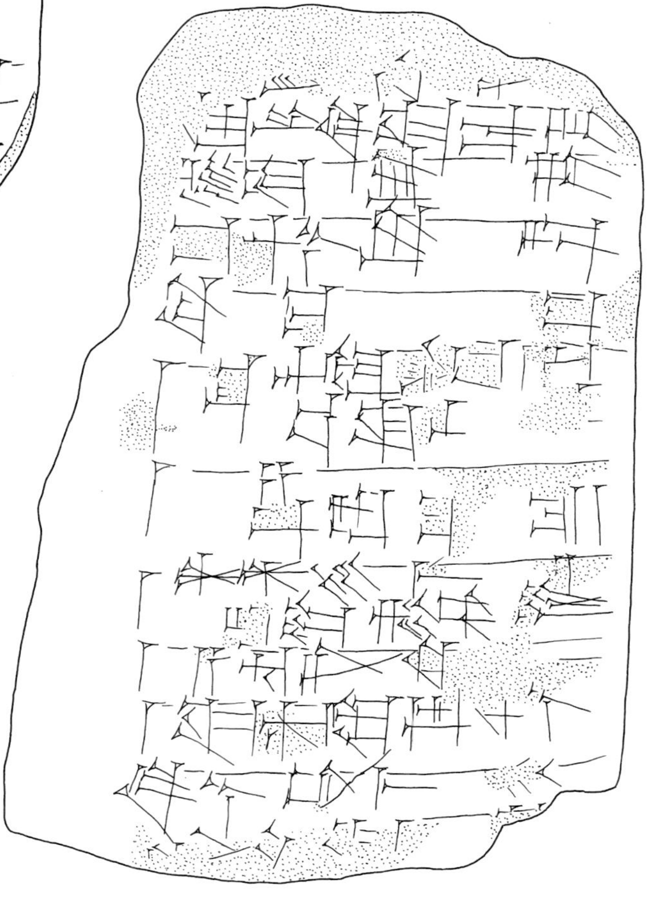

11

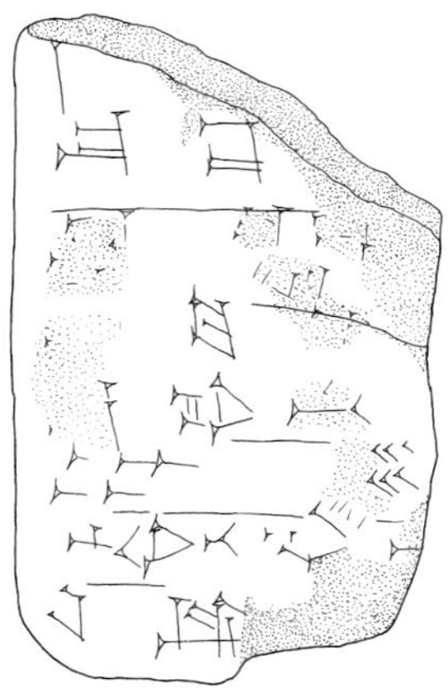

1

Side A

1

Side B

1

Side C

1

Side D

Side A 2 Side B

Side A 3 Side B

Obv. 4

Rev. 4

5

Obv.

5

Rev.

6

Obv.

6

Rev.

7

Obv. Rev.

8

Obv. Rev.

9

Obv.

9

Rev.

10

Obv.

10

Rev.

11

Texte und Materialien der Frau Professor Hilprecht-Collection of Babylonian Antiquities im Eigentum der Friedrich-Schiller-Universität Jena

Herausgegeben von Manfred Krebernik

In der Reihe erscheinen Publikationen von Objekten der Hilprecht-Sammlung im Eigentum der Universität Jena, die größtenteils Keilschrifttexte umfasst, sowie Studien zu einzelnen Objekten und Objektgruppen.

The series comprises publications of objects from the Hilprecht Collection, owned by the University of Jena. For the most part, it consists of cuneiform texts, as well as studies on selected objects and object groups.

6: Johannes J. A. van Dijk, Markham J. Geller

Ur III Incantations from the Frau Professor Hilprecht-Collection, Jena

With the Collaboration of Joachim Oelsner

2003. X, 157 pages, 49 tables, hc
210x297 mm
ISBN 978-3-447-04707-0 *€ 68,– (D)*

This volume contains all of the Sumerian incantations from the time of the Third Dynasty of Ur (ca. 2100–2000 B.C.) housed in the Hilprecht Collection of Near Eastern Antiquities, Jena, along with some related texts from other collections. The edition of this important and difficult corpus of texts, which predominantly stem from the ancient city of Nippur, is based on a manuscript by the famous assyriologist J.J. van Dijk, who died in 1996. Van Dijks posthumous manuscript was revised by Joachim Oelsner and enlarged significantly by Markham J. Geller.
For each cuneiform text the edition provides a transliteration, translation and philological commentary as well as hand copies and photographs. The vocabulary is fully documented in a comprehensive glossary.

7: Christa Müller-Kessler

Die Zauberschalentexte in der Hilprecht-Sammlung

2005. XII, 257 Seiten, 52 Tafeln mit 88 Abb., gb
210x297 mm
ISBN 3-447-05059-4 *€ 68,– (D)*

Der Band vereinigt sämtliche Zauberschalentexte der Hilprecht-Sammlung, Jena. Die allermeisten der mit Beschwörungstexten und z.T. Zeichnungen versehenen, aus Nippur stammenden Keramikschalen werden hier erstmalig veröffentlicht. Die Texte werden in Transliteration und Übersetzung vorgelegt, ausführlich kommentiert und lexikalisch durch ein detailliertes Glossar erschlossen. Alle Stücke sind fotografisch dokumentiert. Zusätzlich zu den 70 Jenaer Stücken wurden parallele Texte anderer Sammlungen (Philadelphia, Istanbul, Bagdad, Chicago, Yale, diverse Privatsammlungen) bearbeitet. Die meisten Schalen sind mit aramäischer Quadratschrift beschrieben, seltener sind syrische Texte in manichäischer Schrift und mandäisch-gnostische Texte. Verhältnismäßig zahlreich ist auch der Anteil von Schalen mit Pseudo-Schriften. Viele Beschwörungen stellen neue Zeugnisse jüdischer Literatur im spätantiken Mesopotamien dar. Zu den herausragenden Texten der Kollektion zählt ein Mezuza-Text sowie eine zweisprachige Interlinearversion des Mose-Liedes Exodus 15:9-12 (hebräisch mit folgendem aramäischen Targum in der Onqelos-Version) als früheste Testimonia aus Babylonien. Bemerkenswert ist eine Textpassage, die sich im Beschwörungskontext des babylonischen Talmud-Traktats Schabbat 67a wiederfindet.

Texte und Materialien der Frau Professor Hilprecht-Collection of Babylonian Antiquities im Eigentum der Friedrich-Schiller-Universität Jena

Herausgegeben von Manfred Krebernik

8: Christine Proust

Tablettes mathématiques de la collection Hilbrecht

Avec la collaboration de Manfred Krebernik et Joachim Oelsner

2008. IX, 166 Seiten, 75 Abb., CD mit Farbscans der Keilschrifttafeln, gb
210x297 mm
ISBN 978-3-447-05705-9 *€ 74,– (D)*

Der Band umfasst Handkopien, Fotografien und Bearbeitungen sämtlicher mathematischen und metrologischen Tafeln der Jenaer Hilprecht-Sammlung (mit Ausnahme des astronomisch-mathematischen „Hilprecht-Textes" HS 245). Die Bearbeitung der mathematisch-metrologischen Texte durch die Mathematikhistorikerin Christine Proust fußt auf langjährigen Vorarbeiten Joachim Oelsners. In die Edition einbezogen sind die auf mehreren Tafeln erhaltenen lexikalischen und literarischen Exzerpte (bearbeitet von Manfred Krebernik). Die Tafeln stammen, soweit nachweisbar, aus Nippur und datieren größtenteils in die altbabylonische Zeit (1. Hälfte des 2. Jahrtausends v.Chr.). Für zwei bereits früher publizierte Texte aus dem 3. Jahrtausend bietet die Neuedition eine Synthese und Aktualisierung der bisherigen Forschung. Die weiteren Texte sind hier zum größten Teil erstmalig publiziert. In einer ausführlichen Einleitung wird das Corpus unter historischen und inhaltlichen Gesichtspunkten vorgestellt und analysiert, wobei neue Aspekte der altbabylonischen Schreiberausbildung und der Rolle der Mathematik innerhalb dieses Curriculums zu Tage treten. Eine Rekonstruktion aller mathematischen Tabellen, ein Glossar der mathematischen Termini sowie Indizes zu den nicht-mathematischen Textabschnitten runden den Band ab. (Text in französischer Sprache)

9: Kai Lämmerhirt

Die sumerische Königshymne Šulgi F

2012. 160 Seiten, 21 Abb., 5 Tabellen, gb
210x297 mm
ISBN 978-3-447-06836-9
⊙E-Book: ISBN 978-3-447-19126-5 *je € 74,– (D)*

Kein anderer mesopotamischer Herrscher wurde so sehr gepriesen wie Šulgi von Ur (2094–2047 v.Chr.). Die zu seinem Ruhm verfassten Hymnen, von denen mehr als 30 ganz oder teilweise überliefert sind, galten schon im antiken Mesopotamien als exemplarische Vertreter der Gattung. Obwohl sich die moderne Forschung intensiv mit Šulgi beschäftigt hat, liegen für viele der auf ihn gedichteten Hymnen bis heute keine modernen Editionen vor. Dies gilt besonders für jene Kompositionen, die wie die Hymne *Šulgi F* einen Umfang von mehr als 300 Zeilen haben.

In *Šulgi F* wird nach einem umfangreichen Aufgabenkatalog für den mesopotamischen Herrscher die Berufung Šulgis durch den Stadtgott Nanna und dessen Reise von Ur nach Nippur geschildert, auf der er beim Hochgott Enlil die Bestätigung des von ihm erwählten Herrschers Šulgi erwirkt. Der Rest der Hymne ist nur fragmentarisch erhalten und ganz dem Preisen des Herrschers gewidmet. Mit Band 9 der „Texte und Materialien der Frau Professor Hilprecht Collection of Babylonian Antiquities" wird die zwischen Hymnus und Epos oszillierende Dichtung erstmals auf der Grundlage sämtlicher bislang bekannter Texte vollständig ediert, übersetzt und kommentiert. In einer ausführlichen Einleitung werden zudem ein grundlegender Forschungsbericht und eine Inhaltsangabe der Dichtung gegeben und Datierungsfragen sowie der „Sitz im Leben" diskutiert.

10: Anne Goddeeris

The Old Babylonian Legal and Administrative Texts in the Hilprecht Collection Jena

With a contribution by Ursula Seidl
Part 1: Texts, Seal Impressions, Studies
Part 2: Indexes, Bibliography, Plates

2016. 2 volumes: 1: XIV, 374 pages, 2: VIII, 313 pages, 1 CD-ROM, incl. 145 plates, hc
210x297 mm
ISBN 978-3-447-10651-1 *€ 198,– (D)*

During the Old Babylonian period (ca. 1900–1700 BC), Nippur, the religious capital of Babylonia, was a center of cultural and economic activities. Excavations have yielded, beside numerous literary compositions, a variety of documents concerning urban and temple administration as well as economic activities and property management of the priestly families.

The book contains the publication of the legal and administrative documents from Old Babylonian Nippur kept in the Hilprecht Collection, Jena. The edition provides transliterations, translations, commentaries, hand copies, and photographs (on CD-ROM) of all texts. The indexes comprise personal names, toponyms, professions, deities, year-names, and a glossary. A separate chapter by Ursula Seidl discusses the iconography of seal impressions on the tablets. The legal documents are keystones of the family archives excavated by the Babylonian Expedition. The book also includes a discussion of the activities related in these archives and of the families who kept them. The administrative documents predominantly belong to a single archive and are characterized by an unusual dating system. The archive keeps track of sections of the management of the city and its temples.